# The Data Detective's Toolkit

## Cutting-Edge Techniques and SAS® Macros to Clean, Prepare, and Manage Data

Kim Chantala

sas.com/books

The correct bibliographic citation for this manual is as follows: Chantala, Kim. 2020. *The Data Detective's Toolkit: Cutting-Edge Techniques and SAS® Macros to Clean, Prepare, and Manage Data*. Cary, NC: SAS Institute Inc.

**The Data Detective's Toolkit: Cutting-Edge Techniques and SAS® Macros to Clean, Prepare, and Manage Data**

SAS Institute Inc., SAS Campus Drive, Cary, NC 27513-2414

December 2020

# Contents

# About This Book

## What Does This Book Cover?

Data professionals who survived deep cuts in funding during the financial crisis of 2007–2008 had to develop innovative methods of data preparation. This book presents innovative data tools and techniques that helped data managers, practitioners, and programmers survive these challenges by reducing the cost and time needed for data management while improving the quality of data prepared with their use. These tools include SAS macros as well as ingenious ways of using SAS procedures and functions.

## Is This Book for You?

This book is designed to help automate many of the tasks performed to turn raw data into analysis-friendly data. These tasks are often filled with a mix of irksome and strenuous activities that stand between you and data that can be used. This book will help preparers of the data in different ways:

| | |
|---|---|
| Intermediate and Advanced users: | You will reduce your workload and improve the quality of your data by using the SAS macro programs included with this book to automate error-checking and create documentation for your project data. Using these programs included with this book will alleviate the tedious nature of data preparation by automating the identification of inconsistencies and anomalies in raw data. |

| Novice users: | If you are not familiar with SAS and are just starting to work with data, you will need to get help from a more experienced programmer to use the SAS macro programs that automatically produce codebooks, reports highlighting problems in the data, inventories of available data sets, and crosswalks showing commonalities of multiple data sets. These are covered in Chapters 3 through 6. Once the SAS statements are set up to run the SAS programs producing these reports, you will find it easy to assist in the detective work of data preparation. Examining these reports will really help you get to know your data, and you can help to solve problems identified in the data. Focusing on the discussion of the output in examples of this book will help you learn to interpret these reports and lead to a better understanding of your data. Skip the sections in each chapter titled "Inside the Toolkit" that discuss the macro program statements in detail. |
|---|---|
| Data managers and Research staff: | You will be able to choose from the many automated reports that function as roadmaps into your data, snapshots of data quality and monitoring, and use these reports to improve communication between your programmer, practitioners, and the data collection sponsors. |
| All users: | No matter what your level of experience, you should read Chapter 1, "Advantages of Using the Data Detective's Toolkit" and Appendix A, "Your Part in the Data Life Cycle." |

## What Are the Prerequisites for This Book?

Familiarity with SAS programming (the DATA step and basic rules of the SAS language) as well as manipulating SAS data with procedures such as PROC CONTENTS, PROC MEANS, and PROC FREQ provide adequate prerequisites for working with the SAS programs and techniques discussed in this book. Familiarity with basic features of the SAS macro language would be useful to run the SAS macro programs that accompany this book. For programmers new to the SAS macro language, detailed instruction is provided in Chapter 2 with information about using SAS.

# What Should You Know about the Examples?

## Software Used to Develop the Book's Content

The output in this book was created with SAS 9.4. Most programs in this book can be run using BASE SAS on the platform that you typically use. A few of the examples use procedures found in the SAS/STAT software.

## Example Code and Data

All data used in the examples in this book was simulated. Any resemblance to actual data sets is purely coincidental. Errors and other anomalies were purposely added to the data to illustrate special features described in this book to clean, prepare, and perform quality control checks on your data.

You can access the example code and data for this book by linking to its author page at https://support.sas.com/chantala.

## Output and Graphics

All output in this book was created with the SAS Output Delivery System. Your output might look slightly different because changes in the appearance of some tables have occurred during the formatting of this book.

# We Want to Hear from You

SAS Press books are written *by* SAS Users *for* SAS Users. We welcome your participation in their development and your feedback on SAS Press books that you are using. Please visit sas.com/books to do the following:

- Sign up to review a book
- Recommend a topic
- Request information about how to become a SAS Press author
- Provide feedback on a book

Do you have questions about a SAS Press book that you are reading? Contact the author through saspress@sas.com or https://support.sas.com/author_feedback.

SAS has many resources to help you find answers and expand your knowledge. If you need additional help, see our list of resources: sas.com/books.

Learn more about this author by visiting her author page at
http://support.sas.com/chantala. There you can download free book excerpts, access
example code and data, read the latest reviews, get updates, and more.

# About the Author

**Kim Chantala** is a Programmer Analyst in the Research Computing Division at RTI International with over 25 years of experience in managing and analyzing research data. Before joining RTI International, she was a data analyst at the University of North Carolina at Chapel Hill. In addition to providing data management and analytical services at the University, she taught workshops on analyzing survey data, focusing on the problems of sample weights and design effects. Kim believes that the real challenge in data analysis is bridging the gap between raw or acquired data and data that is ready to analyze. This inspired her to develop computerized data management tools revolutionizing the way data is prepared, allowing users to improve the quality of their data while lowering the cost of data preparation.

Kim earned a BS in Engineering Physics from the Colorado School of Mines and an MS in Biometrics from the University of Colorado.

Learn more about this author by visiting her author page at http://support.sas.com/chantala. There you can download free book excerpts, access example code and data, read the latest reviews, get updates, and more.

# Acknowledgments

RTI International has generously provided support and resources for me to write this book and enhance the accompanying SAS macro programs. This has allowed me to modernize data preparation efforts and bring these solutions to the attention of the research community. I would like to express my very great appreciation for the RTI infrastructure and expertise which provided a perfect environment for writing this book in addition to testing and developing SAS macro programs that can help you improve the quality of your data while keeping your project on time and within budget. Although early versions of the macro programs in the *Data Detective's Toolkit* were developed while I was employed at UNC, RTI projects have provided larger and more complex data preparation endeavors to test and further develop my macro programs.

Many people have contributed to this book, both knowingly and otherwise. It is not possible to name them all, but I would be remiss in not thanking the following people:

- Jim Terry, Applications Programmer at UNC Chapel Hill, who collaborated in developing the first version of the TK_codebook.sas macro. This early version was released under the name of proc_codebook.sas.

- Jean Robinson, Manager of Systems and Programming at RTI International, for her willingness to share her expertise in project management and developing SAS applications.

- Helen Savage, Director of Operations at RTI International, for general inspiration and moral support.

- Judy Kovenock, past Director of Research Services at the Carolina Population Center at UNC Chapel Hill, for her insight in requiring research programmers to clean and prepare the data that they were responsible for analyzing. She always ended up with meticulous data that was usable and ready for research.

- Many members of the faculty, graduate students, and research staff at UNC Chapel Hill who were willing to use early versions of my SAS macro programs for data preparation. They provided copious amounts of feedback and testing of these macro programs.

- Francesca Florey Eischen, Director of Research Development and Communications at Duke University, for her willingness to share her expertise in research development and project management. Her comments on Appendix A "Your Part in the Data Life Cycle" were insightful and contributed to making the narrative applicable to projects of all complexities.

- Paul Grant (retired), Kim Wilson, Kathryn McLawhorn, and Russ Tyndall from SAS Institute Inc. who tested my SAS code and critiqued my original manuscript.

The SAS Press team has been of the utmost importance in bringing this book to life. I would like to thank the entire team for their tenacity and professionalism in helping me finish this book. I have the good fortune to interact with the following members while writing this book.

- Suzanne Morgen, developmental editor at SAS Institute Inc., who worked with me on writing this book and was a joy to work with. She has really moved this book along and provided the guidance in making my ideas flow and accessible to readers.

- Catherine Connolly, copy editor at SAS Institute Inc., who improved the readability of this book by focusing on the details as well as the big picture.

- Denise Jones, who had the difficult task of getting many of the custom tables produced by my software to conform to the requirements of the publication template.

Of course, all remaining errors in this book are my responsibility.

# Chapter 1: Advantages of Using the Data Detective's Toolkit

## Introduction

You will find the right data tools in this book for creating project data that is ready for exploration and analysis. Using these tools will reduce the amount of time needed to clean, edit, validate, and document your data. Advantages of using the techniques in this book include:

- Accomplishing more while doing less by automating and modernizing the typical data preparation activities

- Beginning at the end by creating research-ready data sets and documentation early in the project with continual updates and improvements throughout collection and preparation

- Keeping the sponsor or lead research investigators engaged by providing codebooks, crosswalks, and data catalogs for review early in the project, thus including them as part of quality control surveillance for the data

This book includes a set of SAS macro programs that automate many of the labor-intensive tasks that you perform during data preparation. Using these macro programs will help guard against compromising quality control and documentation efforts due to rigid project budgets and timelines. You will be able to automate producing codebooks, crosswalks, and data catalogs. Innovative logic built into these macro programs computerizes monitoring the quality of your data using information from the formats and labels created for the variables in your data set. You will receive concise reports identifying invalid data – such as out of range values, missing data, redundant, or contradictory data.

You only need to create a SAS data set with labels and formats assigned to each variable to use these macro programs. It could not be easier or faster to create data that you can trust. The SAS macro programs accompanying this book are available at no charge and can be downloaded from the author page for this book at support.sas.com/chantala.

In the following chapters, you will learn how to use these macro programs to make your job easier and create higher quality data. This chapter introduces you to the macro programs accompanying this book and highlights how they can help solve many of the problems that you face in data preparation.

# An Overview of the *Data Detective's Toolkit*

Data preparation is a heroic task, often with inconsistencies and anomalies in raw data that you must resolve to make the data usable. Your job will include:

- Investigating unexpected or missing values
- Resolving conflicting information across variables
- Mitigating incorrect flow through skip patterns
- Examining incomplete data
- Combining multiple data sets with different attributes
- Documenting changes in data collection methods or instruments during collection

Reconciling these issues requires careful investigation and alleviation during data cleaning and preparation. Rapid advancement in software for both data collection and analysis has encouraged more complex data to be collected. This has caused greater challenges for you as the programmer responsible for turning it into high-quality, research-friendly data. Advances in software to help you solve these issues has progressed at a slower pace than advances in software for analysis or collecting data. This lag in development of computerized tools for data preparation has motivated the development of the macro programs included with this book.

These macro programs have been developed to help you work more efficiently when preparing data and automate much of the tedious work in identifying and correcting problems in your data. Table 1-1 lists the macro programs provided with this book and what they will do for you.

Table 1-1: List of Macro Programs in the *Data Detective's Toolkit*

| Macro Data Tool | Function |
| --- | --- |
| %TK_Codebook | Create codebook, monitor data quality, and identify problems in variables that need further investigation |
| %TK_inventory | Create a catalog showing the inventory of all SAS data sets in a folder |

| Macro Data Tool | Function |
| --- | --- |
| %TK_xwalk | Create a crosswalk table used to show the relationship of variables across a group of data sets |
| %TK_find_dups | Find records with duplicate identification variables in a data set |
| %TK_harmony | Harmonize two data sets with varying file formats, variable naming conventions, data types, labels, and formats |
| %TK_skip_edit | Analyze skip patterns to identify contradictory responses, incorrect flow through prescribed skip pattern, and recode incorrect responses |
| %TK_max_length | Dynamically create the list of variables with maximum storage lengths needed for the LENGTH statement when you are merging or concatenating two data sets |

The only requirement for using these data tools is creating SAS data sets with formats and labels assigned to each variable. Once you have the SAS data set created, you will only need a simple line of SAS code to invoke each of the data tools. The first three macro programs create useful documentation for your data sets. You can create them at the beginning of the project and benefit by having them available for everyone in your team.

## %TK_codebook

The first tool, %TK_codebook, creates a codebook. This macro uses one statement requiring only that you provide the name and location of your SAS data set, the library for the formats assigned to the variables, and a name for your codebook as shown below:

```
%TK_codebook(lib=work,
        file1=test,
        fmtlib=library,
        cb_type=XLSX,
        cb_file=&WorkFolder./Test_CodeBook.xlsx ,
        var_order=internal,
        cb_output = my_codebook,
        cb_size=BRIEF,
        organization = One record per CASEID,
        include_warn=YES);
```

It could not be easier to create a codebook for your data set. But the best feature is yet to come! %TK_codebook will also examine each variable and print informative reports about potential problems. Using information from the label and format assigned to each variable, the %TK_codebook macro warns your data team about variables having the following problems:

- Values missing from the assigned format
- Out of range values
- Missing labels
- No assigned format
- Having 100% missing values
- No variation in the response value

For each variable automatically examined, you would have to write several SAS statements and examine multiple tables to figure out which variables need further examination. If your data set has 1000 variables, you will write SAS statements to create over 2000 tables, examine each table manually to identify problems, then summarize the problems that need investigation. With the reports from %TK_codebook, you are presented with a concise summary of only those variables needing close examination and why they need examination. You will spend your time correcting problems rather than writing repetitive SAS code and examining piles of SAS output. Chapter 3 teaches you how to use %TK_codebook to create a codebook and potential problem reports. These reports identify variables having the problems listed earlier in this section. Chapter 4 teaches you how to customize your codebook in both appearance and adding additional information about variables to the data used to create a codebook.

## %TK_inventory

A catalog of all the SAS data sets for your project can be created at any time during the data life cycle with %TK_inventory by simply providing the full path name of the folder where the data sets reside:

```
libname SAS_data "/Data_Detective/Book/SAS_Datasets";

%TK_inventory(libref=SAS_data);
```

For each data set in the folder associated with libref SAS_data, %TK_inventory will provide information about the following characteristics:

- Data set name
- Data set label
- Creation date
- Number of observations
- Number of variables

This catalog provides a concise summary of the data sets and where they are located, providing an ideal document for communicating a listing of available data. It makes it easier for you and your team to track the progression of developing your data sets. Chapter 5 teaches you how to use the %TK_inventory macro tool.

## %TK_xwalk

The %TK_xwalk tool creates a data crosswalk to help you identify equivalent variables in multiple data sets as well as differences in the attributes of variables having the same name in more than one data set. Again, you only need to use one short statement with a list of data files for %TK_xwalk to create your crosswalk.

```
%TK_xwalk(SetList = SAS_Data.studya SAS_Data.demog SAS_Data.health);
```

This statement creates a mapping of variables across two or more distinct data sets. Reviewing the crosswalk will help you identify variables used to merge the data as well as avoid truncating values when merging or concatenating data sets. You will learn to use %TK_xwalk in Chapter 5.

## %TK_find_dups

You will need to examine each data set verifying that variables uniquely identifying an observation occur only on one observation. You will need to do this on every data set that is created, possibly each time changes are made to program creating your data set. With just a few strokes of the keyboard %TK_find_dups will easily do this for you:

```
%TK_find_dups(dataset=work.STUDY, one_rec_per=CASEID*WAVE,
        up_output=STUDY_DUPS);
```

The output from %TK_find_dups includes the following:

- Table showing the number of observations having identical values of the unique identification variables (CASEID*WAVE)
- Table showing the values of the identification variables that are duplicated across observations.
- Output data set with values of duplicated identification variables that you can use to extract the duplicated observations from your data set.

Chapter 6 teaches you how to use %TK_find_dups.

## %TK_harmony

The %TK_harmony macro can identify possible problems with merging or concatenating two data sets. It is very simple to use, requiring only one statement providing the names of the data sets being harmonized, and nicknames for each data set used in the harmony report created by the %TK_harmony.

```
%TK_harmony(set1= SAS_data.demography_a1,
        set1_id=Web,
        set2= SAS_data.demography_a2,
        set2_id=Paper,
        out=harmony_results);
```

%TK_harmony compares the two data sets and creates a report with the following information:

- Variables unique to each set
- Variables with the same name having different labels
- Variables with the same name having different data types or lengths

You will learn to use the %TK_harmony macro and the output tables in Chapter 6.

## %TK_skip_edit

Skip patterns are used in data collection to ensure that only relevant questions are asked each person participating in the survey. For example, your study might have a set of questions that are asked only of female participants. Male participants would have missing values for all of these questions.

The %TK_skip_edit macro can be used to validate skip patterns as follows:

- Validate that a variable follows the expected pattern of nonmissing/missing values when the variable is part of the skip pattern logic
- Handle special recoding to correct inconsistencies in skip patterns and help users understand why a variable is missing

For example, suppose question PG1 asks women the number of pregnancies they have had in their lifetime. This would not be asked if the participant was male. Question DEM2 in the survey asks each participant their sex (1=female, 2=male). %TK_skip_edit uses this information to examine this skip pattern for you and change the value of PG1 to missing if a male responded to that question. You only need to set up a format identifying the values of a variable that cause a SKIP, and then pass this information to TK_skip_edit:

```
proc format;
    value SKIP2f 2='2=SKIP';
run;
%TK_skip_edit(check_var = PG1,
    skip_vars = DEM2,
    skip_fmts = DEM2 skip2f.);
```

%TK_skip_edit produces an annotated table reporting results from analyzing data flow through the skip pattern and any edits that were made to the data to resolve inconsistencies in the data flow. You will learn more about skip patterns and how to use the %TK_skip_edit macro in Chapter 7.

## %TK_max_length

SAS prints the following message in your log file to warn you that there is a mismatch in the storage length of variables in the data sets being combined in a DATA step:

```
WARNING: Multiple lengths were specified for the variable VAR_NAME by
input data set(s). This can cause truncation of data.
```

When you see this message, it means that the values stored in VAR_NAME were possibly truncated when the data sets were combined with a MERGE or SET statement. To prevent this from happening, you can use the %TK_max_length macro to create a macro variable named &MAX_LENGTHS that contains information about the variables common to two data sets but have different storage lengths. This list includes the name and the longest defined length of each variable. Macro variable &MAX_LENGTHS can be used in the LENGTH statement in the DATA step to prevent truncation of data values when two data sets are combined. The SAS statements below show how easy it is to use %TK_max_length and a LENGTH statement to prevent truncating data values:

```
%TK_max_length(set1=My_Data.teleform_data, set2=My_data.web_data);

data survey_v2;
length &max_lengths;
set My_Data.teleform_data My_Data.web_data;
run;
```

You will learn more about using the %TK_max_length in Chapter 2.

## Summary

This chapter explained the benefits of using this book for data cleaning, preparation, and management. Using these macro programs reduces the time needed to prepare data that you can trust. You will automate creating documentation for your data by easily creating codebooks, crosswalks, and data catalogs with just a few strokes on the keyboard. The way you clean data will be modernized enabling you to easily to detect, investigate, and correct inaccurate data values in your data set.

The strength of using these macro programs to automate cleaning data and creating documentation lies in their general applicability and simplicity of use. The only requirement for you to use them is having a SAS data set with labels and formats assigned to the variables.

You will use these tools in every stage of the life cycle of your data. Read Appendix A to understand more about the data life cycle. You will read about the common activities in every stage of the data life cycle, learning how your data flows through each stage from inception of the idea to acquire your data through archival at project end. You will find useful checklists showing recommended tasks for cleaning, using, distributing, and archiving your data.

# Chapter 2: The Data Detective's Toolkit and SAS

## Introduction

In this chapter you will learn SAS programming features needed to understand the examples in this book and to automate data cleaning and report generation using the SAS macros from this book. You will discover:

- How to prepare a SAS data set with embedded metadata needed by the SAS macro programs from the *Data Detective's Toolkit*

- Fundamental concepts of the SAS macro programming language needed to run the macro SAS programs and customize reports

- How to use the Output Delivery System to obtain data sets from SAS procedures and to create reports or files in the Microsoft Excel, Microsoft Word, or Adobe Reader format.

## Preparing Your SAS Data Set

One of the most beneficial features of SAS is the facility to store useful information with each variable in a SAS data set. This type of information about a variable or data set is called metadata. Metadata is data about other data. SAS also automatically stores helpful information (metadata) about the data set at the time it is created or when the metadata of a SAS data set is changed. The SAS macro programs in the *Data Detective's Toolkit* use this metadata to create codebooks, crosswalks, and master data set lists. This metadata is also used to automate data cleaning, error detection, and quality control.

This section provides instruction on adding metadata to a SAS data set so that you get the most benefit from using the *Data Detective's Toolkit* when you prepare your data set. You create this metadata by using SAS statements to easily add text descriptions to variables, their values and data sets.

## Types of Metadata

The metadata stored with your SAS data set and used by the *Data Detective's Toolkit* can be classified into three categories as listed below:

- Descriptive metadata describing the meaning and values of your variables
- Structural metadata describing the structure of your data set such as number of observations and number of variables
- Administrative data describing attributes of a data set when it was created, including information such as date created, file type, protection, and data set label

Having this information included as part of the data makes each SAS data set self-contained and self-documenting. This section describes how you can use SAS to create three types of descriptive labels that can be assigned to the following:

- The SAS data set (Administrative metadata)
- Each variable in the data set (Descriptive metadata)
- The data values in those variables (Descriptive metadata)

Nearly all the structural and administrative metadata is created by SAS when the data set is created, but it can also be added, updated, or changed after the data set is created.

## Using SAS to add Metadata to Your Data Set

It is easy to create a data set with the metadata needed to automate data cleaning and report generation with macro programs from the *Data Detective's Toolkit*. After the overview describing the flow of the program in Example 2-1, you will find instructions on storing metadata with each variable by creating and storing formats and labels with your own data sets.

### Example 2-1: Adding Metadata to your SAS data set

Program 2-1 is an example of a program preparing a data set to be used with macros from the *Data Detective's Toolkit*.

**Program 2-1: Program to Add Formats and Labels to a SAS Data Set**

```
/* DEFINE FOLDER TO WRITE SAS DATA SET*/
libname My_Data "/Data_Detective/Book/SAS_Datasets";

/* STEP 1) Create formats to define meaning of values for each variable*/
proc format;
    value $anytext " "="Missing (blank)" other="Data present";
    value $showall default = 40 " "="Missing (blank)";
    value race      1 = "White"
                    2 = "Hispanic"
                    3 = "Black"
```

```
       4 = "Asian";
    value sex 1="Male" 2="Female";
    value days 1-7="Valid Range" -99="Presented, not answered (web only)";
run;

/* STEP 2) Create a data set */
data My_Data.HWS (label="Final Data for Healthy Worker Study");
    set My_Data.StudyA_raw;

    /* STEP 3) Assign a format to each variable in data set*/
    format race race.;
    format int_date mmddyy10.;
    format sex sex.;
    format sick_days days.;
    format comment $anytext.;
    format clinic $showall.;

    /* STEP 4) Assign labels to variables in data set*/
    label race = "Race/Ethnicity";
    label int_date = "Interview date";
    label sex = "Sex of participant";
    label sick_days = "Days absent due to illness past week";
    label comment = "Text description of illness";
    label clinic = "Name of Clinic";
run;
```

A SAS program consists of global statements that set up the processing environment for your program, a DATA step that consists of programming statements to create, import, or modify variables and save in a data set, and the PROC step, which consists of procedure statements to analyze SAS data sets.

Global statements can be used anywhere in your program and include statements to do the following:

- Create comments that will be ignored by the SAS processor

- Define titles and footnotes for your output (TITLE and FOOTNOTE statements)

- Set up system options to tailor the processing of your program (OPTIONS statement)

- Define folders (LIBNAME statement)

- Capture output from SAS procedures and create reports with special formatting (Output Delivery System (ODS) statements)

- Define macro variables used to perform symbolic substitutions when your SAS job is executing

The SAS processor identifies comments as any text enclosed by an asterisk (*) and ends with a semicolon (;), or any text that begins with the two characters /* and ends with swapping those two characters */ . Examples of valid comments appear below:

> \* Comment text appears here ;

> /* Comment text appears here */

COMMENT statements occur at several places in the example program. If you are writing a SAS macro program, comments in the form of /* comment */ are the safest comments to use inside a macro. This ensures that the macro processor recognizes your COMMENT statement as a comment rather than part of a statement that needs to be expanded into a SAS statement.

The LIBNAME statement in the example SAS code is used to assign a nickname to the folder where you will write your SAS data set.

A PROC step begins with a PROC statement and ends with a RUN or QUIT statement, another PROC statement, or a DATA statement. PROC FORMAT (Step 1) in the example is an illustration of a PROC step and is used to create a custom format that can be used to associate a meaningful description to the values that can occur for one or more variables.

Next a DATA step (Step 2) creates a SAS data set named MY_DATA.HWS stored in the folder assigned to nickname "MY_DATA" by the LIBNAME statement. Use the SAS data set option "LABEL=" to assign a text description ("Final data for the Healthy Worker Study") that will be stored with the data set. Within the DATA step you can define the metadata describing each variable in the data set. To do this, you assign a format (Step 3) to each variable that specifies a character string used when printing the value of the variable, and assign a label (Step 4) to each variable defining the meaning of the variable.

## Specifications for Creating Formats and Labels

This section provides a general review of the syntax and options available to create formats and labels for the variables in your data set. More details can be found in the SAS documentation.

### Create Formats (Step 1)

PROC FORMAT can be used to create informative labels assigned to a value or range of values for a variable. You can assign a text description to each value or range of values for a variable by using the VALUE statement in PROC FORMAT. The VALUE statement has the form:

```
value <$>fmt_name <format-option(s)> value-range-set(s);
```

The name of the format (fmt_name) can be 32 characters for numeric variables. For character variables, the first character for the name of the format must be a $ followed by up to 31 characters in length (fmt_name).

The *format-option(s)* include arguments to specify default, minimum or maximum length of a format and a fuzz factor for matching values to a range. See the SAS documentation for more information.

The *value-range-set(s)* enable you to assign a text description up to 32,767 characters to a value or set of values. The text description must be enclosed in single or double quotation marks.

Below are a few example formats that can be useful for creating a codebook.

```
proc format;
value $anytext ' '='Missing (blank) other='Data present';
value $showall (default = 40) ' '='Missing (blank)' ;
value month 1-12 = "Valid range" -99='Not answered';
run;
```

The $anytext format can be assigned to a character variable that does not have meaningful category descriptions. This allows the data to be summarized in only three categories (Missing (blank), Period (.), and Data Present). This is a useful format for open-ended text or names or other identifying information that you prefer to appear summarized as one category in the codebook.

The $showall format is useful to assign to character variables if you prefer that every unique value of the variable appears in the codebook. The default = 40 in the value specification indicates to display a maximum of 40 characters. If any values have more than 40 characters, they will be truncated so be sure the number specified as the default length is large enough to accommodate formatted values for this variable.

The month format is an example of creating a format defining the valid range for a variable. This type of format is useful for numeric variables that you want to display with a range of values rather than meaningful categories.

Although the code below is syntactically correct, the macro programs included with this book require that the descriptions assigned to a value in the value-range-sets be unique. For example, the format status has two different values assigned to the value label "Complete":

```
proc format; /* Do not use: format has duplicated descriptions*/
value status
    2720 = "Web Survey started"
    2799 = "Complete"
    2820 = "Phone survey contact"
    2899 = "Complete";

proc format; /* Do not use: format has duplicated descriptions */
value status
    2720 = "Web Survey started"
    2799,2899 = "Complete"
    2820 = "Phone survey started";
```

To keep the status values 2799 and 2899 as separate categories, add information to the value labels so that each label is unique as shown in the following method of writing the format. This creates a format that works well for the data tool macros.

```
proc format; /* Use: Value descriptions that are unique */
value status
    2720 = "Web Survey started"
    2799 = "Web Survey completed"
    2820 = "Phone Survey started"
    2899 = "Phone Survey completed";
run;
```

## SAS Date Formats

The %TK_codebook macro program included with this book recognizes certain date-time formats assigned to a variable and display the range (minimum to maximum) of their values in the codebook that it creates. The following date time formats are recognized:

- DATETIME: Any format beginning with DATETIME displays the minimum and maximum "date part" of the variable using an mmddyy10. format.

- MMDDYY: Any format beginning with MMDDYY displays the minimum and maximum dates with the assigned date format.

- TIME: Any format beginning with TIME displays the minimum and maximum time values with the assigned time format.

## Add Label to Data Set (Step 2)

A DATA step is where data is created, modified, and combined with other sets, and where calculations are performed and metadata are assigned. The DATA step begins with a DATA statement and ends with a RUN statement, another DATA step, or a PROC step. The DATA step begins with a DATA statement where you can use the LABEL= option to assign and store a text string description of up to 256 characters to a SAS data set. You can use this to provide additional information or a description stored with your data set. This label is used by the SAS macro programs included with this book to provide additional information about the data set in the reports produced. Below is an example of assigning a label to a data set named MY_DATA.HWS:

```
data MY_DATA.HWS (label="Final data for Healthy Worker Study");
```

## Assign Formats (Step 3)

Formats created with the VALUE statement in PROC FORMAT can be permanently assigned to one or more variables. To do this, assign the name of the format created by a VALUE statement to a variable using the FORMAT statement in a DATA step. Using the SAS code shown below, you can create a data set called "final" from a data set called "clean" and assign a format to each variable.

```
data final;
set clean;
```

```
format final_status status.;
format name $anytext.;
format month month.;
format city $showall.;
run;
```

The FORMAT statements assign one of the formats created by the VALUE statements in the PROC FORMAT step that we covered earlier in Step 1. Note that a period (.) comes immediately after the name of the format in each of the statements so that SAS understands that this is the name of the format and not another variable.

### Variable Labels (Step 4)

The SAS LABEL statement is used to assign a text description to each variable in the data set:

```
label variable_name = "Description";
```

The LABEL statement is used in the DATA step to assign a text description that is saved with a variable as the data set is being created. The description can be up to 256 characters in length and should be enclosed in single or double quotation marks.

If you only want to change the metadata of variables (that is, modify labels, formats, etc.) in an existing data set, then it is much more efficient to use PROC DATASETS to make these changes. The simple code shown above unnecessarily rereads all the data. But as in the earlier example code, where you are creating a new data set with a MERGE, adding these variable attributes in the same DATA step is the right way to go.

You should now be able to prepare your data set with embedded metadata including variable labels, variable formats, and a data set label. This information is used by the macro programs included with this book to automate data cleaning and creating documentation. This section covered only relevant features of SAS statements used in the examples in this book. Additional information about these SAS statements is available in the online SAS documentation located at http://support.sas.com/.

## Fundamental SAS Macro Concepts

This section provides an overview of the SAS Macro language emphasizing what you need to know to run the SAS macro programs included in the *Data Detective's Toolkit*. You will learn the following basic macro programming skills used in the examples in this book:

- Setting macro system options
- Creating and using macro variables
- Running SAS macro programs

You will need to understand these three tasks to follow the examples in this book and use the macros in the *Data Detective's Toolkit* for preparing your own data.

To provide a deeper understanding of the SAS Macro language, this section also introduces the knowledge that you need to write your own macro programs or investigate the SAS macro programs in the *Data Detective's Toolkit*. You will find a summary of the macro processing features used in developing the SAS macros in the *Data Detective's Toolkit* that include:

- Controlling flow of program logic
- Special SAS macro variables
- Macro language statements and functions

Although you can skip this summary, it will be useful if you want to learn more advanced SAS macro programming techniques by studying the "Inside the Toolkit" description for each macro data tool presented in the following chapters. This section concludes with explaining how these macro concepts were used to create one of the macro programs in the *Data Detective's Toolkit*.

## What is the Macro Language?

The SAS macro language enables you to create a program that the SAS processor expands into a sequence of SAS statements to do repetitive or common tasks. In its simplest form, a macro program acts like a run-time text editor, enabling you to automatically substitute text in SAS programming statements to create a stream of SAS commands when running your program. No permanent changes are made in the original macro program. You can easily create simple macro programs by identifying portions of your SAS code that you need to frequently use, or when you have sections of your code that need to be changed a little then reused. Your macro program can also control the flow of your SAS statements by using the macro language to define a conditional sequence for your statements.

The SAS macro language includes system macro variables and statements that add to the flexibility of creating your own macro programs. Note that each system macro variable begins with SYS. You should avoid creating a macro variable that begins with the 3-letter prefix, SYS. The SYS prefix is reserved by SAS for automatically creating macro variables to supply a variety of information about your SAS job.

The system macro variables used in this book provide the current date information and are shown in Table 2-1.

**Table 2-1: SAS Macro Date Variables**

| Variable | Contains | Example |
|---|---|---|
| SYSDATE | Date a SAS job began running, stored as a character value (2-digit year) | If today is March 10, 2020, then &SYSDATE = 10MAR20 |
| SYSDATE9 | Date a SAS job began running, stored as a character value (4-digit year) | If today is March 10, 2020, then &SYSDATE9 = 10MAR2020 |

| Variable | Contains | Example |
|---|---|---|
| SYSDAY | Day of the week that the SAS job began running | If today is Tuesday, then &SYSDAY = Tuesday |
| SYSTIME | Time a SAS job or session began running, stored as a character value | If the time is 4:42 pm, then &SYSTIME =16:42 |

These system variables are useful to automate updating the name of a data set being created each night, or update dates in titles of reports being created. There are many other SAS macro variables available to provide information about the processing of your SAS job.

In your SAS program, macro variables are always referenced by using the "&"as a special prefix allowing the SAS processor to differentiate them from SAS variable names occurring in your data.

A list of the macro statements that you will find used in this book appears in Table 2-2. Italics indicate text that you supply, such as the name of a macro program.

**Table 2-2: SAS Macro Language Statements Used in This Book**

| Type | Macro Statement | Function | Where used[1] |
|---|---|---|---|
| Assign value | %LET *MacroVarName*= | Assign value to macro variable | O, M |
| | PROC SQL; SELECT <*VarName*> INTO: <*MacroVarName*> | Assign values from variable to macro variable | O, M |
| | CALL SYMPUTX(*MacroVarName, value*); | Assign a value to a macro variable | O, M |
| Access macro variable | %GLOBAL *MacroVar* | Allows access to macro variable in main program and all macro programs | O, M |
| | %LOCAL *MacroVar;* | Allows access to macro variable in only the program where it was created | M |

| Type | Macro Statement | Function | Where used[1] |
|------|-----------------|----------|---------------|
| Invoke macro | %*macro_name* | Runs the macro program named macro_name | O, M |
| Define macro program | %MACRO *macro_name* | Indicates the beginning of a macro program | O, M |
| | %MEND; | Indicates the end of a macro program | O, M |
| Comment | %* *comment* ; | Macro comment statement | O, M |
| | /* *comment* */ | Comment statement | O, M |
| Control flow of program logic | %DO<br>%DO %UNTIL<br>%DO %WHILE<br>%IF *condition* %THEN<br>%IF *condition* %THEN %DO | Begins a conditional sequence of code | O[2] M |
| End flow of program logic | %END; | Ends a conditional sequence of code | M |
| Write to SAS log | %PUT | Writes messages to SAS log | O, M |

1) M indicates statement is valid within a macro program, O indicates the statement is valid in open code (code that is not part of a macro program)

2) %IF/%THEN/%DO is valid in open code starting at SAS9.4M5.

Macro commands always begin with a % sign. A macro statement will always end with a semicolon. These two characters, & and %, are triggers for the macro language processor to convert the macro statement into the SAS language before your code is executed.

The special option keywords available in the OPTIONS statement that enable you to view the SAS statements generated when your macro program is executed are listed in Table 2-3. Many other macro options are available for macro processing.

### Table 2-3: SAS Options for Macro Processing

| Option Keyword | Function |
| --- | --- |
| MPRINT | Lists the SAS statements generated by macro execution in the SAS log file |
| MLOGIC | Requests the macro processor to trace its execution and write trace information to the SAS log. Useful when debugging your macro program |
| MFILE | Directs the output from MPRINT to a file |
| SOURCE2 | Requests SAS write source statements from files that have been included by %INCLUDE statements to the SAS log |
| SYMBOLGEN | Lists the values of the SAS macro variables in the log file |

The next section will help you understand how to use these statements by showing you how to use one of the macros in the *Data Detective's Toolkit* and then investigate how it works.

## Using the *Data Detective's Toolkit* Macro Programs

This section uses a simple macro from the *Data Detective's Toolkit* to illustrate how you use the SAS commands from Tables 2-1 to 2-3 to run a macro from the *Data Detective's Toolkit*. After learning how to run the macro, you will have the opportunity to go inside the macro and learn how it works. In this section, you will learn:

- SAS statements that you need to know to understand the examples in this book
  - Print SAS statements generated by the macro processor
  - Create macro variables that identify the full path of a folder
  - Use SAS date variables as part of your title statements
  - Include a SAS macro program as part of your program code
  - Run a SAS macro from your program
- Details of how a SAS macro program is constructed
  - Defining the beginning and ending of a macro program with SAS statements
  - Passing parameter values to the macro program

- ○  Creating global macro variables
- ○  Examining macro information printed to the log file

## Example 2-2: Fixing Truncation of Data Values When Combining Data Sets

In this example, you discover the unfortunate consequences of combining two different data sets that have variables with the same name but different *storage* lengths. The storage length is the number of bytes used to store the values of each variable in a SAS data set. You will learn how easy it is to use the %TK_max_length macro program to fix the problem that occurs.

You have been asked to concatenate two data sets for a survey currently being collected. The first data set (teleform_data) is created by scanning information filled out on a paper form, and the second data set (web_data) is created by a web-based data collection application. Each of these data sets has four variables with the same name.

Below is the simple SAS program that you write to concatenate the two sets:

```
libname My_Data "/DataDetective/Examples/Data ";

data all_survey_v1;
set my_data.web_data my_data.teleform_data;
run;
```

Checking the log file, you find this message:

```
WARNING: Multiple lengths were specified for the variable state by input
data set(s). This can cause truncation of data.
```

You get this WARNING when combining the data sets with the SET, MERGE, or UPDATE statement if any of the variables having the same name and type in the data sets have different storage lengths. This can cause truncating of values (character variables) or loss of precision (numeric variables).

One way to investigate this WARNING is to use PROC CONTENTS to examine the storage length of each variable and PROC PRINT to list observations from the data sets.

```
proc contents data=my_data.web_data;
title "Web Data";
run;
proc print data=my_data.web_data;
var id city state source;
run;
```

Shown below in Output 2-1 is a portion of the information printed by PROC CONTENTS, followed by a listing of observations from the web data.

**Output 2-1: Output to Examine Variables in Web Data**

*Web Data*

### The CONTENTS Procedure

| Data Set Name | MY_DATA.WEB_DATA | Observations | 7 |
|---|---|---|---|
| Member Type | DATA | Variables | 4 |

| Alphabetic List of Variables and Attributes | | | |
|---|---|---|---|
| # | Variable | Type | Len |
| 1 | city | Char | 11 |
| 4 | id | Num | 8 |
| 3 | source | Char | 6 |
| 2 | state | Char | 2 |

| Obs | id | city | state | source |
|---|---|---|---|---|
| 1 | 10 | PUEBLO | CO | WEB |
| 2 | 11 | ANKORAGE | AK | WEB |
| 3 | 12 | MOBILE | AL | WEB |
| 4 | 13 | BLOOMFIELD | MI | WEB |
| 5 | 14 | MINNEAPOLIS | MN | WEB |
| 6 | 15 | HATTIESBURG | MS | WEB |
| 7 | 16 | SPRINGFIELD | MO | WEB |

Next, PROC CONTENTS and PROC PRINT are used to obtain similar information from the TELEFORM data. The output from these statements is shown in Output 2-2.

```
proc contents data=my_data.teleform_data;
title "Paper (teleform) Data";
run;
proc print data=my_data.teleform_data;
title "Paper (teleform) Data";
var id city state source;
run;
```

## Output 2-2: Output to Examine Variables in the Teleform Data Set

*Paper (teleform) Data*
*The CONTENTS Procedure*

| Data Set Name | MY_DATA.TELEFORM_DATA | Observations | 4 |
|---|---|---|---|
| Member Type | DATA | Variables | 4 |

**Alphabetic List of Variables and Attributes**

| # | Variable | Type | Len |
|---|---|---|---|
| 1 | city | Char | 11 |
| 4 | id | Num | 8 |
| 3 | source | Char | 6 |
| 2 | state | Char | 11 |

*Paper (teleform) Data*

| Obs | id | city | state | source |
|---|---|---|---|---|
| 1 | 20 | ALLEN | MICHIGAN | PAPER |
| 2 | 21 | DULUTH | MINNESOTA | PAPER |
| 3 | 22 | TUPELO | MISSISSIPPI | PAPER |
| 4 | 23 | JOPLIN | MISSOURI | PAPER |

Finally, the entire data set is printed. The listing of the observations is shown in Output 2-3.

```
proc print data=all_survey_v1;
title "Concatenated data -- all_survey_v1";
var id city state source;
run;
```

## Output 2-3: Listing Showing Truncated Values of Variable State

*Concatenated data -- all_survey_v1*

| Obs | id | city | state | source |
|---|---|---|---|---|
| 1 | 10 | PUEBLO | CO | WEB |
| 2 | 11 | ANKORAGE | AK | WEB |
| 3 | 12 | MOBILE | AL | WEB |
| 4 | 13 | BLOOMFIELD | MI | WEB |

| Obs | id | city | state | source |
|-----|----|------|-------|--------|
| 5 | 14 | MINNEAPOLIS | MN | WEB |
| 6 | 15 | HATTIESBURG | MS | WEB |
| 7 | 16 | SPRINGFIELD | MO | WEB |
| 8 | 20 | ALLEN | MI | PAPER |
| 9 | 21 | DULUTH | MI | PAPER |
| 10 | 22 | TUPELO | MI | PAPER |
| 11 | 23 | JOPLIN | MI | PAPER |

Comparing the output from both of the PROC PRINT steps shows that the two-letter state abbreviation is used for the value of variable "STATE" in the web data, but the entire name of the state is used for the value of "STATE" in the Paper (TELEFORM_DATA) data. Looking at the concatenated data from data set "ALL_SURVEY_V1" shows that names stored in variable STATE were truncated to just two characters. This is because SAS uses the variable attributes from the data set that is listed first (MYDATA.WEB_DATA) in the SET or MERGE statements. Unfortunately, the data from the Paper (TELEFORM_DATA) data now appears to all be from the same state MI (Michigan).

You can find out the lengths of the state variable by examining the output from PROC CONTENTS, which shows all variables and their attributes. From this output, you can determine that variable STATE has a length of 2 characters in the web data but a length of 11 characters in the TELEFORM data. To assign a common length to variable STATE from the two data sets, you would add a LENGTH statement preceding the SET, MERGE or UPDATE statement in your DATA step as shown below:

```
data all_survey_v1;
length STATE $11;
set my_data.web_data my_data.teleform_data;
run;
```

This would fix the truncation error for variable STATE when combining the two sets. The pitfall with doing this investigative work to find the right lengths and hardcoding it into your DATA step is that this same error might occur the next time you have to combine the files. This is because the lengths of the variables in the input data sets might have been updated to accommodate new data. For example, the TELEFORM data might include surveys from states with names that have more than 11 characters, such as Massachusetts or North Carolina. You would need to repeat your investigative work and modify the LENGTH statement in your program to prevent truncating the data. You might also start having a similar problem with values of the CITY and SOURCE variables being truncated. An easier and more robust way to correct the error is to use the %TK_max_length macro to dynamically create the list of variables with maximum lengths needed for the LENGTH statement every time you combine the sets.

Program 2-2 shows the SAS code that you would use to run the %TK_max_length macro program to create the LENGTH statement with the variable specification(s) needed to merge the two data sets without truncating values of any of the variables.

## Program 2-2: Using %TK_max_length to Prevent Truncating Data Values When Combining Data Sets

```
/* Options to print SAS statements & values of macro variables to log */

options mprint symbolgen;

/* Create macro variables for the names of the folders needed for data and
SAS include files*/

%let DataFolder=/Data_Detective/Book/SAS_Datasets;
%let TKFolder= /Data_Detective/Book/SAS_programs/TK_toolkit;

/* THE FOLLOWING STATEMENTS ARE REQUIRED */

libname My_Data "&DataFolder";

%include "&TKFolder/TK_max_length.sas";

%TK_max_length(set1=My_Data.teleform_data, set2=My_data.web_data);

data survey_v2;
length &max_lengths;
set My_Data.teleform_data My_Data.web_data;
run;

proc print data=survey_v2;
title "Survey_v2 data for date: &sysdate9 at &systime";
var id city state source;
run;
```

This code uses many of the SAS macro programming features covered in this section. The OPTIONS statement requests that all SAS statements generated by the macro (OPTION MPRINT) and the value of any macro variables used in the processing (OPTION SYMBOLGEN) be written to the log file. This is useful for debugging or understanding a macro program.

The %LET statements create macro variables that contain the name of folders used later in the program.

The LIBNAME statement is needed for reading the data sets since they are permanent SAS data sets stored in folders on disk. The macro variable &DATAFOLDER is used in the LIBNAME statement rather than entering the entire folder name. Inspecting the SAS log, you would find this statement generated by the SAS processor when the program is ran:

```
SYMBOLGEN: Macro variable DATAFOLDER resolves to
/Data_Detective/Book/SAS_Datasets
NOTE: Libref MY_DATA was successfully assigned as follows:
    Engine:         V9
    Physical Name: /Data_Detective/Book/SAS_Datasets
```

The %INCLUDE statement brings in the SAS code for %TK_max_length into your SAS program. The macro variable &TKFOLDER is used in place of the folder in the path name of the

%TK_max_length macro. The SAS log provides this information to show how the %INCLUDE statement was resolved:

```
SYMBOLGEN:  Macro variable TKFOLDER resolves to
            /Data_Detective/Book/SAS_programs/Ch2_examples
36
37          %include "&TKFolder/TK_max_length.sas";
```

Rather than using the macro variable &TKFolder to provide the name of the folder, you can enter the full path name of the %TK_max_length macro program to include the macro program with your program.

The next statement:

```
%TK_max_length(set1=My_Data.teleform_data, set2=My_data.web_data)
```

runs the %TK_max_length macro program. No printed output is produced from this macro, but it creates a macro variable named &MAX_LENGTHS containing a list of all the variables in the two sets with the same name and type but differ in storage length. The name of each variable listed in &MAX_LENGTHS will be followed by the maximum storage length needed for that variable. This is used in a LENGTH statement to combine the two sets without truncating the value of the variable.

The general form and explanation of the code that you need to run %TK_max_length is shown below:

**Macro Syntax**

%TK_max_length(set1=*SetName1*, set2=*SetName2*)

**Required Keyword Parameters**

set1:    Name of first data set being combined

set2:    Name of second data set being combined

Using the % sign as a prefix to the name of a macro program tells the SAS processor to execute the macro program. Inside the parenthesis are the macro parameters that are passed into the macro at invocation. Within the macro program code, each parameter name has the & sign prepended as prefix (that is, &set1) when it is used. Every time the SAS processor finds a parameter in the macro code (that is, &set1) the processor will substitute the value assigned to the parameter (that is, *SetName1*) to create the actual statements that are executed.

When you write a macro program you can use two types of parameters: positional and keyword. With positional parameters, you can omit the parameter name and just specify the value of the parameters within the parenthesis following the *%macro_name* invocation. However, you must list these values in the same order as they are in the macro program definition.

All the macro programs in the *Data Detective's Toolkit* are written to use only keyword parameters when they are run. The macro parameters (set1 and set2 used in %TK_max_length) are defined as keyword parameters rather than positional parameters within the macro program. When using keyword parameters, you must specify the name of the macro parameter (such as set1), an equal sign (=), followed by the value that you want the parameter to take on (such as My_Data.teleform_data) within the macro code. Keyword parameters can be listed in any order and can also be assigned a default value within the macro program definition.

When the %TK_max_length macro finishes running, it will have created a macro variable named &MAX_LENGTHS that contains the name and maximum number of bytes (the length) for variables that have different lengths in the two data sets. During execution, MPRINT from the OPTIONS statement causes the generated SAS statements to be written to the log file showing how the macro code is interpreted at run time. This part of the SAS log file will be covered in the next section where you will explore how the %TK_max_length program is made.

After the macro finishes running, the DATA step that follows uses the &MAX_LENGTHS macro variable to concatenate the two data sets creating the data set named survey_v2. Below are statements from the log file showing the details of the processing:

```
180          data survey_v2;
SYMBOLGEN:  Macro variable MAX_LENGTHS resolves to      STATE $ 11
181          length &max_lengths;
182          set My_Data.teleform_data My_Data.web_data;
183          run;
```

A statement beginning with SYMBOLGEN was written to the log file because SYMBOLGEN was listed in the OPTIONS statement earlier in the program. We see that the %TK_max_length macro found that only the variable STATE has different lengths in the two data sets, and that 11 bytes was the maximum length.

The PROC step that follows uses the PRINT procedure to show what the concatenated data set contains. Output 2-4 shows the observations in the data set created and verifies that no truncation of values has occurred.

**Output 2-4: Listing Showing the Correct Values of Variable State**

*Survey_v2 data for date: 11OCT2020 at 16:09*

| Obs | id | city | STATE | source |
|---|---|---|---|---|
| 1 | 20 | ALLEN | MICHIGAN | PAPER |
| 2 | 21 | DULUTH | MINNESOTA | PAPER |
| 3 | 22 | TUPELO | MISSISSIPPI | PAPER |
| 4 | 23 | JOPLIN | MISSOURI | PAPER |
| 5 | 10 | PUEBLO | CO | WEB |
| 6 | 11 | ANKORAGE | AK | WEB |
| 7 | 12 | MOBILE | AL | WEB |
| 8 | 13 | BLOOMFIELD | MI | WEB |
| 9 | 14 | MINNEAPOLIS | MN | WEB |

| Obs | id | city | STATE | source |
|-----|-----|------|-------|--------|
| 10 | 15 | HATTIESBURG | MS | WEB |
| 11 | 16 | SPRINGFIELD | MO | WEB |

The SAS log file shows the following statements that created the table listing data from the survey_v2 data set:

```
184
185          proc print data=survey_v2;
SYMBOLGEN:  Macro variable SYSDATE9 resolves to 11MAY2020
SYMBOLGEN:  Macro variable SYSTIME resolves to 14:10
186          title "Survey_v2 data for date: &sysdate9 at &systime";
187          var id city state source;
188          run;
```

The SYMBOLGEN entries in the SAS log file show the values of the SAS system variables SYSDATE9 and SYSTIME that were substituted into the TITLE statement.

### Inside the Toolkit: %TK_max_length Macro

This section explores the %TK_max_length macro to show many of the features of the SAS language presented in the general discussion of the SAS macro language. This section is optional and is not needed for being able to use the SAS macros in the *Data Detective's Toolkit*, but it will be helpful if you want to write your own macro programs or modify the %TK_max_length macro program. This macro will automatically perform the steps that you needed to do by hand to find the maximum length of the STATE variable to fix the truncation problem in the original SAS program:

- Run PROC CONTENTS to determine the length of STATE variable in the web data set

- Run PROC CONTENTS to determine the length of STATE variable in the teleform data set

- Compare output from each PROC CONTENTS to determine the maximum length of variable STATE

- Create a text string with the maximum length for the STATE variable and store that text string in a macro variable to use with a LENGTH statement in the DATA step combining the web and teleform data sets

The %TK_max_length macro program uses another macro program, %get_length, to determine the length of all variables in a data set. Program 2-3 shows the SAS macro statements from %TK_max_length followed by statements from the %get_length macro program.

**Program 2-3: The %TK_max_length and %get_length Macro Program Source Code**

```
/* Macro %TK_max_length */

%macro TK_max_length(set1=, set2=);

%get_length(set=&set1, out=_tk_out1_, length=length1, type=type1 );
```

```
%get_length(set=&set2, out=_tk_out2_, length=length2, type=type2 );

data _tk_lengths_;
merge _tk_out1_ _tk_out2_;
by name;
   /* type = 2 means character variable, type = 1 means numeric variable */
if type1=2 and type2=2 and (length1 ne length2) then
  length_info=compress(Name) || ' $ ' || compress(max(length1, length2));
else if type1=1 and type2=1 and (length1 ne length2) then
  length_info=compress(Name) || ' ' || compress(max(length1, length2));
run;

%global max_lengths;
%let max_lengths=;

proc SQL noprint;
Select length_info into :max_lengths separated by ' '
  from work._tk_lengths_;
quit;

proc datasets noprint ;
  delete _tk_out1_ _tk_out2_ _tk_lengths_;
run;

%mend ;

/* Macro %get_length */

%macro get_length(set=, out=, length=, type= );
proc contents data=&set noprint out=&out(keep=name type length);

data &out;
set &out;
name=upcase(name);
rename length=&length;
rename type=&type;
run;

proc sort data=&out;
by name;
run;

%mend ;
```

This code includes two macro programs that are used to create the macro variable
&MAX_LENGTHS needed for the LENGTH statement that will correct the truncated data error.
These macros are:

- The %TK_max_length macro:
  - Beginning with statement %macro TK_max_length(set1=, set2=);
  - Ending with statement %mend;

- The %get_length macro:
    - Beginning with statement %macro get_length(set=, out=, length=, type= );
    - Ending with statement %mend;

The first two statements of the %TK_max_length macro use the %get_length macro to obtain information about the variables in each data set.

The %get_length macro does the following:

- Uses PROC CONTENTS to get the name, length, and data type for all variables in a data set and stores this information in a data set named by the out= keyword parameter
- Prepares this data set for merging with another data set created by another invocation of the %get_length macro
    - Makes the variable names all uppercase and renames the length and type of the variable to names defined in the parameter list for the %get_length macro
    - Sorts the data set by the variable NAME

The %TK_max_length macro has used the %get_length macro to obtain the following information about each variable in each data set specified in the keyword parameters SET1 and SET2:

- Variable name
- Variable length
- Data type

Next, a DATA step is used to compare the storage lengths of variables that have the same name and data type in the two files. This DATA step creates an output data set (_tk_lengths_) having the information needed for the LENGTH statement stored in a variable called LENGTH_INFO.

Next the %TK_max_length macro creates a global macro variable (&MAX_LENGTHS) initialized to a null value that is available to all programs ran during a SAS session or job. PROC SQL is used to fill the value of &MAX_LENGTHS macro variable by reading all values of the variable LENGTH_INFO and transposing those values into one row separated by a comma. The global macro variable is now ready for use anywhere in the SAS job.

If all variables are common to both files and have the same length, then a null value is created for the value of the &MAX_LENGTHS macro variable and will be used in the LENGTH statement in the DATA step in Program 2-2. The code generated by the SAS macro processor would be:

```
length ;
```

The last task that the %TK_max_length does is to use PROC DATASETS to clean up its workspace by deleting the data sets created by this macro (_tk_out1_, _tk_out2_, and _tk_lengths_).

# The Output Delivery System

SAS provides the Output Delivery System (ODS) so you can easily capture the reports from SAS procedures or user-written macros and save it in a file. These reports can be formatted for display using a variety of popular software applications including Microsoft Word, Microsoft Excel, and Adobe Acrobat. You can also customize the appearance of the report contents and presentation. The macros provided with this book have not been tested using PowerPoint as the destination for the ODS.

The examples in this book use the ODS system to direct the output from the Toolkit macros to create files with reports formatted for Word, Excel, and Adobe Acrobat. These examples explain how to customize the reports by changing colors, fonts, and borders. The basic form of the ODS statements that you will see in the examples creating formatted reports is shown below:

```
ods destination file="filename" style=style-definition <option(s)> ;

* SAS procedure code to create report appears here;

ods destination close;
```

The *destination* tells the ODS driver what output format should be used to create your report. The following table shows some of destinations available for ODS.

**Table 2-4: Partial List of ODS Destinations**

| Destination | Function |
| --- | --- |
| RTF | Create file formatted written in Rich Text Format for use with Microsoft Word |
| EXCEL | Use to transfer data or report into Microsoft Excel |
| PDF | Create file formatted for Adobe Acrobat |
| HTML | Create file for use on the worldwide web |
| XML | Produce file with plain text data interchange format |
| PostScript | Create file for printing purposes |
| Listing | Uses plain text for output |
| Output | Create an output data set from the ODS tables produced by SAS procedures |

The Destination name on the first six rows of the previous table specifies the type formatting to use when creating the output report. Special formatting such as colors, fonts, and borders is handled by assigning a template (*style-definition*) to the *style* option in the ODS statement. The *style-definition* is the name of a template available with SAS or one you create with PROC TEMPLATE. You will learn more about using PROC TEMPLATE in Example 4.3 in Chapter 4.

The last destination (output) listed in Table 2-4 is used to obtain output data sets from the ODS tables produced by SAS procedures. Use the following statement to find out the *output-object-name* for all ODS tables created by a SAS procedure:

```
ods trace on;

* SAS procedure code appears here;

ods trace off;
```

The *output-object-name* for all ODS tables created by the SAS procedure will be written to the log file. After examining the log file to determine which table you want saved as an output data set, use the following form of ODS statement to save the ODS table as a SAS data set:

```
* SAS procedure code appears here;

ods output output-object-name = my-data-set_name;
```

The following chapters have many examples using ODS to get an output data set.

## Summary

The same basic steps can be used to run every macro program in the *Data Detective's Toolkit* and are listed below.

- Set up the macro system options
    - Include the MPRINT option to see SAS statements created from the macro code (optional)
    - Include SYMBOLGEN option to see values of macro variables when they are referenced (optional)
    - Create any SAS macro variables to define folders or file names (optional) that you will reference in your main SAS program
- Set up processing options for your SAS job
    - Use OPTIONS statement to define orientation, margins, and other characteristics for your report
    - Define TITLE statements
    - Create LIBNAME statements
    - Include the Toolkit macro program as part of your program code

- Prepare your SAS data set
  - Use PROC FORMAT to create formats
  - Use a DATA step to create SAS data set or PROC DATASETS to modify an existing SAS data set
    - Add a label to the SAS data set
    - Assign formats to the variables
    - Assign labels to the variables
- Run the Toolkit macro program
  - Use an ODS statement to save the output as formatted report (optional)
  - Run the SAS macro program using keyword parameters to pass values to the macro
  - Use an ODS close statement to close the formatted report (optional)

You now are ready to run the macros included with this book.

# Chapter 3: Codebooks: A Roadmap to Your Data

## Introduction

Codebooks provide a roadmap for using your data and are as important as the data itself. With a good codebook, users of your data are able to answer many questions about the data without actually accessing the data set. With the best codebooks, both you and users of your data will see the reality of what is in your data set rather than what someone planned to include or thought it would contain.

This chapter describes what you will find in the best codebooks, how to use that information, and how to create a codebook by using the %TK_codebook macro. In addition to creating a codebook, you will experience using the most powerful feature of the %TK_codebook macro to effortlessly perform quality control checks, such as identifying variables that have out of range values, missing labels, incomplete format definitions, and no variation in their values. At the end of this chapter, you will be taken inside the programming of the %TK_codebook macro and shown how the metadata stored within your data set is used to produce a codebook displaying complete and self-explanatory information for each variable, as well as automate quality control checks on each variable.

## Understanding Codebooks

Codebooks are essential to understanding and using a data set. They provide information about the structure of the data set, when it was created, and the meaning of every variable and their values. Information describing the main purpose of the study, sampling information, and technical information are often written in a separate manual or as a separate section preceding the actual codebook. This information is so important to choosing the correct way to analyze the data that the data preparation team might choose to provide a short synopsis of it as part of the codebook itself.

Shown in Codebook 3-1 is part of a codebook that illustrates features found in the best of codebooks. In this codebook, information about the data set is included in a header appearing at the top of the page. First, the main purpose of the data is listed in the first thee lines of text and describes who collected or created the data as well as why and how the data was collected. Technical Information appearing on the next four lines documents the name and label of the SAS data set, the creation date, and the number of observations and variables in the data set. The last line of text provides information about how the data set is organized relative to the primary sampling unit.

By examining information about the variables in your codebook, the sponsor, lead researchers, and your analysis team will be able to determine whether the data meets the research criteria established for collecting the data or the needs for their analysis. This part of the codebook describes the variables in your data and provides information about the assigned format and data type. The descriptive statistics or frequency distribution of variables provides estimates of the sample population represented by the data or the prevalence of the observed factors and outcomes of the study. You can see that CASEID is a numeric variable distinguishing a record for a particular participant. It has no missing values and ranges in values from 10,000 to 10,500. The second variable, CITY, tells where the participant lives and is a character variable containing a value up to 20 characters in length. The distribution of participants from each city shown in the Frequency and Percent columns lets you know the distribution of participants from each city. The third variable, RACE, shows the racial distribution of the participants in your sample.

You will learn how to create a codebook like this one in the next section.

## Codebook 3-1: Example Codebook

*Master Codebook for Study A Instructional Data Created for the Data Detective*
*Data Simulated as a Simple Random Sample for Participants in a Health Study*
*Data Created for Illustrating the Data Detective's Toolkit*

*Data Set: StudyA.sas7bdat*
*Label: Simulated Data for Study A*
*Date Created: 30MAY20:16:56:12*
*Number of Observations: 501     Number of Variables: 5*
*Organization of Data Set: One record per Participant (CASEID)*

| Variable Name | Label | Format | Type | Mean | Values | Frequency Category | Frequency | Percent | Cumulative Frequency | Cumulative Percent |
|---|---|---|---|---|---|---|---|---|---|---|
| CASEID | Unique identifier for participant | | Num 8 | 10250 | . | SAS missing (.) | 0 | 0.00 | 0 | 0.00 |
| | | | | | 10000 to 10500 | Range | 501 | 100.00 | 501 | 100.00 |
| BIRTHDATE | Date of birth | MMDDYY10.0 | Num 8 | 07/15/1979 | . | SAS missing (.) | 45 | 8.98 | 45 | 8.98 |
| | | | | | 05/28/1967 to 03/30/1992 | Range | 456 | 91.02 | 501 | 100.00 |
| SEX | Sex of participant | SEX | Num 8 | 1.50 | 1 | Male | 249 | 49.70 | 249 | 49.70 |
| | | | | | 2 | Female | 252 | 50.30 | 501 | 100.00 |
| RACE | Race/Ethnicity | RACE | Num 8 | 1.80 | . | SAS missing (.) | 30 | 5.99 | 30 | 5.99 |
| | | | | | 1 | White | 270 | 53.89 | 300 | 59.88 |
| | | | | | 2 | Hispanic | 47 | 9.38 | 347 | 69.26 |
| | | | | | 3 | Black | 130 | 25.95 | 477 | 95.21 |
| | | | | | 4 | Asian | 24 | 4.79 | 501 | 100.00 |
| CITY | Fictional city where participant lives | $SHOWALL | Char 20 | | Emerald Falls | Emerald Falls | 179 | 35.73 | 179 | 35.73 |
| | | | | | Garnetville | Garnetville | 83 | 16.57 | 262 | 52.30 |
| | | | | | New Diamond | New Diamond | 141 | 28.14 | 403 | 80.44 |
| | | | | | Ruby | Ruby | 98 | 19.56 | 501 | 100.00 |

# Using the %TK_codebook Macro

You can easily create a codebook with the %TK_codebook macro. It is simple to use, requiring only the following information:

- Titles for the codebook
- A SAS data set that has labels and formats assigned to the variables
- A format catalog defining the formats assigned to the variables
- Full path name and type (PDF, XLSX, RTF, or HTML) of the codebook being created

You can also request the following reports listing potential problems identified in the data:

- Incomplete formats
- Out of range values
- No variation in response values
- Variables not assigned a user-defined format
- Variables missing labels

The %TK_codebook macro uses information stored within the SAS data set to create the codebook and potential problem reports. You control this information by defining the data set label, each variable label and format assigned to the variable. The previous chapter, "The *Data Detective's Toolkit* and SAS," describes how to do this and suggests ways of creating formats to help provide the most information for the %TK_codebook macro to make your codebook.

## Syntax

The %TK_codebook macro can be run with the following statement:

```
%TK_codebook(lib = libname_data,
        file1 = data_set_name,
        fmtlib = libname_formats,
        cb_type = type_keyword,
        cb_file=codebook_name,
        organization = data_set_organization,
        cb_size=size_keyword,
        var_order=order_keyword,
        include_warn=warn_keyword,
        cb_output=output_data_set);
```

### Required Keywords

| | |
|---|---|
| LIB= | Name of library for SAS data set (for FILE1 variable) |
| FILE1= | Name of SAS data set used to create the codebook |
| FMTLIB= | Name of format library |

| | |
|---|---|
| CB_TYPE= | Type of codebook (XML, XLSX, PDF, RTF) |
| CB_FILE= | Name of file for the codebook being created |

**Optional Keywords**

ORGANIZATION=    Text indicating the organization of observations in the data set. For example, there might be one record per CASEID or one record per CASEID*WAVE. In this example, CASEID (unique identification number for participant) and WAVE (interview number) are variables in the data set used to create a codebook.

CB_SIZE=    Flag to control size of codebook by limiting the number of columns of information about each variable in codebook.

- BRIEF requests reduced size
- FULL requests complete listing

See section on output data set for information about variables in FULL and BRIEF codebooks.

VAR_ORDER=    Controls order variables printed in codebook:

- CUSTOM_ORDER (order from file named work.custom_order, see *ORDERING VARIABLES IN CODEBOOK* section of this chapter)
- INTERNAL (order of variables as stored in data set)
- Omitted defaults to alphabetical

INCLUDE_WARN=    Flag to control printing of WARNING messages to reports in codebook (in addition to LOG file)

- YES prints warnings at the end of file specified by CB_FILE (default)
- NO prints warnings only in LOG file

CB_OUTPUT=    Name of output data set created by %TK_codebook macro to create the FULL or BRIEF codebook. See the next section *Output Data Set* for complete list of variables.

## A Word of Caution When Using Excel to Create Your Codebook

Microsoft Excel is an incredibly wonderful program, but it does not understand SAS variable data types and formats when ODS EXCEL is used to format the file. For example, if you have a numeric variable with all numbers and a SAS missing value of period (.), then it sometimes turns that period into a zero (0), which can be really disastrous for your codebook. %TK_codebook looks for all variables that have only numbers and replaces SAS missing values of a period with a blank to safeguard against this happening if you use ODS Excel Unfortunately, you might also have data values with leading zeros and Excel will drop the leading zeros. Examples of these types of variables include Social Security Numbers, ZIP codes, ICD-10 codes, and possibly variables comprised of only numbers used to uniquely identify individuals. To prevent this, you can use CB_TYPE=XML to create a codebook with HTML. This tells the %TK_codebook macro to use ODS TAGSETS.ExcelXP to format your codebook. When this happens, special formatting instructions included with the PROC REPORT statements that print the codebook will interpret the values correctly. The XML file that is created will be very large. After the XML file is created, open it with Excel and save as an Excel file. More information about this topic can be found in "Creating *AND* Importing Multi-Sheet Excel Workbooks the Easy Way with SAS®" by Vincent DelGobbo, available at https://support.sas.com/resources/papers/proceedings/proceedings/sugi31/115-31.pdf.

## Ordering Variables in Codebook

The VAR_ORDER option enables you to have the variables in the codebook listed alphabetically (default) or as stored in the data set (VAR_ORDER=INTERNAL). If you prefer a different ordering scheme, create a simple two-variable file called work.custom_order before you call the macro. The first variable is NAME, a 32-character field with your variable name in UPPERCASE. The second variable is ORDER, a numeric field with the order in which you want the variables to be printed. An example DATA step creating a work.custom_order data set is shown below.

```
data custom_order;
length name $ 32;
name = "T1";      ORDER = 1; OUTPUT;
name = "HHID09"; ORDER = 2; OUTPUT;
name = "LINE09"; ORDER = 3; OUTPUT;
name = "H1D";     ORDER = 4; OUTPUT;
run;
```

The %TK_codebook macro will look for this data set named "custom_order" if you specify VAR_ORDER=CUSTOM.

## Output Data Set

Each row that you see in the codebook created by %TK_codebook is an observation in this output data set. For example, the variable, CITY, from your project data set will have four records (one record for each of Emerald Falls, Garnetville, New Diamond, and Ruby in Codebook 3-1) in the output data set created by %TK_codebook.

All of the following variables having a value of Yes or No in column 1 in Table 3-1 are used in the CB_SIZE=FULL option and are included in the output data set even if CB_SIZE=BRIEF is requested. The variables ORDER, CNT, and ORDER_FLAG are used by the %TK_codebook macro to control the order the variables and values are listed in the printed codebook. These variables provide the following information used by PROC REPORT in %TK_codebook to determine how rows in the codebook should be printed.

- ORDER is a number that controls the order in which the variables from your project data set are listed in the codebook report. It is determined from the VAR_ORDER= keyword.

- CNT is a number that controls the order the FREQUENCY, PERCENT, CUMFREQUENCY, and CUMPERCENT are listed. These statistics are not computed by PROC REPORT, but come from an output data set created by PROC FREQ and merged with other data about each variable to create the Codebook Output data set.

- ORDER_FLAG is a number that indicates the order the observations are printed in the codebook created by %TK_codebook.

All other variables in the table are listed as columns in the printed codebook.

The variable MEAN_CHAR in the output data set is a character rather than numeric to allow different formats for the mean of each numeric variable in your project data set used to display the value.

Examples in Chapter 4 show you how to use the output data set to customize the appearance of your codebook.

**Table 3-1: Variables in Output Data Set Used to Create Codebook**

| CB_SIZE = BRIEF | VARIABLE | Type | Length | Label |
|---|---|---|---|---|
| Yes | name | Char | 32 | Variable name |
| Yes | order | Num | 8 | Variable number order |
| Yes | desc | Char | 37 | Value label (Frequency Category text description) |
| No | format | Char | 32 | Variable format |
| Yes | label | Char | 256 | Variable label |
| Yes | range | Char | 40 | Values assigned to this category |
| Yes | frequency | Num | 8 | Frequency |

| CB_SIZE = BRIEF | VARIABLE | Type | Length | Label |
| --- | --- | --- | --- | --- |
| Yes | percent | Num | 8 | Percent |
| No | cumfrequency | Num | 8 | Cumulative frequency |
| No | cumpercent | Num | 8 | Cumulative percent |
| Yes | cnt | Num | 8 | Order of value as it would appear in PROC FREQ output |
| No | mean_char | Char | 15 | Mean of values for numeric variable |
| Yes | type_length | Char | 9 | Variable type and length |
| Yes | order_flag | Num | 8 | Requested order of variables and values (RANGE/DESC) categories |
| Yes | set_name | Char | 22 | Data set name |
| Yes | set_label | Char | 34 | Data set label |
| Yes | date_created | Char | 16 | Date data set created |
| Yes | num_obs | Char | 3 | Number of observations in data set |
| Yes | num_var | Char | 2 | Number of variables in data set |

# Example 3-1: Create a Codebook with Potential Problem Reports

In this example, you will learn to create a codebook using the %TK_codebook macro program. The data set used still needs to be cleaned and has problems that will be reported in the potential problem reports created by the %TK_codebook macro. These problems will also be apparent in the codebook, but you will save time by having the %TK_codebook macro find them and list the issues that you need to investigate in the potential problem reports before you have examined every variable in the data set.

The first step is to create a SAS format library for the variables in the data set. Shown in Program 3-1 are the SAS statements that you can use to create a format catalog named formats.sas7bcat and store within the folder /Data_Detective/Book/SAS_data sets.

## Program 3-1: Create Formats for Data Set

```
libname sas_data "/Data_Detective/Book/SAS_Data sets";

proc format library = sas_data.formats;

     value $mode 'PAPI'  = 'Paper and Pencil Personal Interview'
           'CAPI'  = 'Computer Assisted Personal Interview'
           'SAQ' = 'Self Administered Questionnaire'
           'CASI' = 'Computer Assisted Self Interview'
           'TDE' = 'Touchtone Data Entry'
           'VOIP' = 'Web Cam Interview'
           'CAI' = 'Computer Assisted Interview'
           'CATI' = 'Computer Assisted Telephone Interview'
           'WEB' = 'Web Interview';

     value sex 1='Male' 2='Female';

     value race 1 = 'White'
           2 = 'Hispanic'
           3 = 'Black'
           4 = 'Asian';

     value $anytext ' '='Missing (blank)' other='Text or value supplied';

     /* default specifies default length of format for printing */
     value $showall (default = 20) ' '='Missing (blank)';

     /* OTHER prints actual value for all values not equal to SAS missing
value*/
     value shownum . = 'SAS Missing (.)' other = _same_;

     /* OTHER prints 'Any Number' for all values not equal to SAS missing
value*/
     value anymiss .='SAS Missing (.)' other='Any Number';

     value by5s 0='0' 1-5='1-5' 6-10='6-10' 11-15='11-15' 16-20='16-20'
21-25='21-25';

     value by10s 0='0' 1-10='1-10' 11-20='11-20' 21-30='21-30' 31-40='31-
40'
           41-50='41-50' 51-high='51 or more';

     value health 1='Excellent'
           2='Very Good'
           3='Good'
           4='Fair'
           5='Poor';

     value weight 1 = 'Very underweight'
           2 = 'Somewhat underweight'
           3='Healthy weight'
           4 = 'Somewhat overweight'
           5 = 'Very Overweight';
```

```
        value chg_wt 1 = 'Trying to lose weight'
                2 = 'Trying to stay same weight'
                3 = 'Trying to gain weight'
                4 = 'Nothing';
run;
```

Your next step is to read in the raw data and assign formats and labels to variables. You also assign a label to the data set.

### Program 3-2: Prepare Data Set with Formats and Labels

```
libname sas_data "/Data_Detective/Book/SAS_Data sets";
options fmtsearch=(sas_data);  /* Look for formats in catalog in libname
sas_data*/

data SAS_data.StudyA_Prelim (label=Preliminary data for Study A);
    set SAS_data.StudyA_raw;

    format race race.;
    format sex sex.;
    format mode $mode.;
    format health health.;
    format weight weight.;
    format chg_weight chg_wt.;
    format int_date mmddyy10.;
    format birthdate mmddyy10.;
    label language = "Language";
    label caseid = "Unique identifier for participant";
    label birthdate="Date of birth ";
    label race = "Race/Ethnicity";
    label sex = "Sex of participant";
    label health = "How is your health?";
    label weight = "How would you describe your weight?";
    label chg_weight = "What are you trying to do about your weight?";
    label exer_days = "In the Past 30 days, how many days did you exercise
at
         least 30 minutes?";
    label num_doc_visits = "Number of doctor visits in the past year";
run;
```

You are ready to create a codebook. The SAS code to create the codebook appears below. If you want to see the SAS source code created by this macro program, add SOURCE2 and MPRINT to the OPTIONS statement. You can specify one or more titles for your codebook.

### Program 3-3: Create a Codebook with the %TK_codebook Macro

```
title 'Master Codebook for Study A Preliminary Data';
title2 'Simulated Data for Participants in a Health Study';
title3 'Created as a Simple Random Sample';

options papersize=letter orientation=portrait leftmargin=1.5in
rightmargin=1.5in topmargin=1.5in bottommargin=1.5in;
options label nodate nonumber ;

*--------------UPDATE THE FOLLOWING AS NEEDED----------------------------;
%let TKFolder = /Data_Detective/Book/SAS_programs/TK_toolkit;
```

```
%let DataFolder = /Data_Detective/Book/SAS_Data sets;
%let WorkFolder = /Data_Detective/Book/SAS_Output;

libname SAS_data "&DataFolder";

%let cb_name=&WorkFolder/Program3_3_Codebook.rtf ;
%include "&TKFolder./TK_codebook.sas";
*---------------------------------------------------------------------------;

%TK_codebook(lib=SAS_data,
        file1=StudyA_prelim,
        fmtlib=SAS_data,
        cb_type=RTF,
        cb_file=&cb_name,
        var_order=internal,
        cb_output = my_codebook,
        cb_size=FULL,
        organization = One record per CASEID,
        include_warn=YES);
run;
```

Below is an explanation of the information that you specified in the %TK_codebook statement to create your codebook:

- Use the data in /Data_Detective/Book/SAS_Data sets /StudyA_prelim.sas7bdat (file1=StudyA_prelim, lib=SAS_data)

- Use the formats stored in the file /Data_Detective/Book/SAS_Data sets /formats.sas7bcat to find the meaning of the values of the variables in the StudyA_prelim.sas7bdat data set (fmtlib=SAS_data)

- Save the codebook in a file named /Data_Detective/Book/ Program3_3_Codebook.rtf so that we can open it with WORD (cb_type=RTF, cb_file=&cb_name)

- Order the variables listed in the codebook with the same order as they are stored in StudyA_prelim.sas7bdat (var_order=internal)

- Save the data used to create the codebook in a data set named "my_codebook"

- Print all columns in the codebook to Variable Name, Label, Type, Values, Value labels (Frequency Category), Frequency, Percent (cb_size=FULL)

- Include information about the organization of the data set (organization = One record per CASEID)

- Print the potential problem reports (include_warn=YES)

## Interpreting the Codebook

Codebook 3-2 summarizes all observations in the data set named StudyA_prelim.sas7bdat. The first three lines printed in the codebook are created with title statements listed in Program 3-3. Metadata stored with the data set are extracted by %TK_codebook and used to print the technical information that appears next. The name of the data set (StudyA_prelim.sas7bdat) used to create the codebook appears on the first line listed in the technical information section. The next line displays the data label *"Preliminary data for Study A"* that was assigned to

StudyA_prelim.sas7bdat in the DATA step that created it. The remaining lines of the technical information section informs you that this data set was created on June 05, 2020 at 4:42 pm and has 501 observations and 17 variables. The last line in the header indicates the data set has only one record per value of variable CASEID.

Information about each of the 17 variables in the StudyA_prelim.sas7bdat follows the technical information. The records are raw, unweighted counts of the number of responses recorded for each variable. The name of the format assigned to each variable is included in this FULL report but would be omitted from the BRIEF report.

The codebook provides a concise synopsis of your data and will easily show anomalies in a variable that require further investigation. The data set used in this example contains problems to illustrate this process. Examining the information about each variable displayed in Codebook 3-1 identifies the following problems that need to be investigated.

- No format was given for the character variable CITY, so all observations were lumped into one category called "Blank, Text, or Value supplied".

- Variable MODE was assigned a format used to display the value label in the "Frequency Category" for each of the six modes of data collection displayed in the "Values" column.

- No format was assigned to numeric variables CASEID and AGE, so the %TK_codebook macro reported the numeric range and information about the amount of missing values.

- The variables INT_DATE and BIRTHDATE had the SAS format mmddyy10. assigned and the %TK_codebook macro used this information to display the range of values as actual dates rather than numeric values.

- None of the user-defined formats had a category defined for missing, so the %TK_codebook added a category "SAS missing(.)" to the description listed in the "Frequency Category."

- The HEALTH and WEIGHT variables have values that are not defined in the assigned formats. The codebook program lists these undefined values in both the "Value" and "Frequency Category" columns. Variables with undefined values will be listed in the "Incomplete Format" and "Out of Range Value" reports.

These problems will also be summarized in the potential problem reports.

### Codebook 3-2: Codebook with Problems to Illustrate the Potential Problem Reports

*Master Codebook for Study A Preliminary Data*
*Simulated Data for Participants in a Health Study*
*Created as a Simple Random Sample*

*Data Set:  StudyA_prelim.sas7bdat*
*Label:  Preliminary data for Study A*
*Date Created: 05JUN20:16:42:05*
*Number of Observations:  501      Number of Variables:  17*
*Organization of Data Set:  One record per CASEID*

| Variable Name | Label | Format | Type | Mean | Values | Frequency Category | Frequency | Percent | Cumulative Frequency | Cumulative Percent |
|---|---|---|---|---|---|---|---|---|---|---|
| CITY | Fictional city where participant lives | | Char 20 | | **OTHER** | Blank, Text, or Value supplied | 501 | 100.00 | 501 | 100.00 |
| MODE | Mode of data collection | $MODE | Char 4 | | CAI | Computer Assisted Interview | 139 | 27.74 | 139 | 27.74 |
| | | | | | CAPI | Computer Assisted Personal Interview | 32 | 6.39 | 171 | 34.13 |
| | | | | | PAPI | Paper and Pencil Personal Interview | 33 | 6.59 | 204 | 40.72 |
| | | | | | TDE | Touchtone Data Entry | 126 | 25.15 | 330 | 65.87 |
| | | | | | VOIP | Web Cam Interview | 33 | 6.59 | 363 | 72.46 |
| | | | | | WEB | Web Interview | 138 | 27.54 | 501 | 100.00 |
| CASEID | Unique identifier for participant | | Num 8 | 10250 | . | SAS missing (.) | 0 | 0.00 | 0 | 0.00 |
| | | | | | 10000 to 10500 | Range | 501 | 100.00 | 501 | 100.00 |
| INT_DATE | Interview date | MMDDYY 10.0 | Num 8 | 04/05/2017 | . | SAS missing (.) | 0 | 0.00 | 0 | 0.00 |
| | | | | | 03/21/2017 to 04/20/2017 | Range | 501 | 100.00 | 501 | 100.00 |

| Variable | Label | Format | Value | Code | Description | N | Percent | Cum N | Cum Percent |
|---|---|---|---|---|---|---|---|---|---|
| BIRTHDATE | Date of birth | MMDDYY 10.0 | 07/15/1979 | . | SAS missing (.) | 45 | 8.98 | 45 | 8.98 |
|  |  |  |  | 05/28/1967 to 03/30/1992 | Range | 456 | 91.02 | 501 | 100.00 |
| AGE | Age at interview date | Num 8 | 37.24 | . | SAS missing (.) | 45 | 8.98 | 45 | 8.98 |
|  |  |  |  | 25 to 49 | Range | 456 | 91.02 | 501 | 100.00 |
| SEX | Sex of participant | Num 8 | 1.50 | 1 | Male | 249 | 49.70 | 249 | 49.70 |
|  |  |  |  | 2 | Female | 252 | 50.30 | 501 | 100.00 |
| RACE | Race/Ethnicity | Num 8 | 1.80 | . | SAS missing (.) | 30 | 5.99 | 30 | 5.99 |
|  |  |  |  | 1 | White | 270 | 53.89 | 300 | 59.88 |
|  |  |  |  | 2 | Hispanic | 47 | 9.38 | 347 | 69.26 |
|  |  |  |  | 3 | Black | 130 | 25.95 | 477 | 95.21 |
|  |  |  |  | 4 | Asian | 24 | 4.79 | 501 | 100.00 |
| HEALTH | How is your health? | Num 8 | 2.44 | 1 | Excellent | 123 | 24.55 | 123 | 24.55 |
|  |  |  |  | 2 | Very Good | 173 | 34.53 | 296 | 59.08 |
|  |  |  |  | 3 | Good | 116 | 23.15 | 412 | 82.24 |
|  |  |  |  | 4 | Fair | 55 | 10.98 | 467 | 93.21 |
|  |  |  |  | 5 | Poor | 20 | 3.99 | 487 | 97.21 |
|  |  |  |  | 6 | 6 | 14 | 2.79 | 501 | 100.00 |
| WEIGHT | How would you describe your weight? | Num 8 | 2.81 | 0 | 0 | 16 | 3.19 | 16 | 3.19 |
|  |  |  |  | 1 | Very underweight | 86 | 17.17 | 102 | 20.36 |
|  |  |  |  | 2 | Somewhat underweight | 48 | 9.58 | 150 | 29.94 |
|  |  |  |  | 3 | Healthy weight | 211 | 42.12 | 361 | 72.06 |
|  |  |  |  | 4 | Somewhat overweight | 109 | 21.76 | 470 | 93.81 |

| Variable | Description | Name | Type | Mean | Value | Label | Frequency | Percent | Cumulative Frequency | Cumulative Percent |
|---|---|---|---|---|---|---|---|---|---|---|
| | | | | | 5 | Very Overweight | 31 | 6.19 | 501 | 100.00 |
| CHG_WEIGHT | What are you trying to do about your weight? | CHG_WT | Num 8 | 1.66 | . | SAS missing (.) | 54 | 10.78 | 54 | 10.78 |
| | | | | | 1 | Trying to lose weight | 265 | 52.89 | 319 | 63.67 |
| | | | | | 2 | Trying to stay same weight | 107 | 21.36 | 426 | 85.03 |
| | | | | | 3 | Trying to gain weight | 39 | 7.78 | 465 | 92.81 |
| | | | | | 4 | Nothing | 36 | 7.19 | 501 | 100.00 |
| EXER_DAYS | In the Past 30 days, how many days did you exercise at least 30 minutes? | | Num 8 | 17.24 | . | SAS missing (.) | 0 | 0.00 | 0 | 0.00 |
| | | | | | 0 to 34 | Range | 501 | 100.00 | 501 | 100.00 |
| SMOKE | Do you currently smoke? | | Num 8 | 0.28 | . | SAS missing (.) | 0 | 0.00 | 0 | 0.00 |
| | | | | | 0 to 1 | Range | 501 | 100.00 | 501 | 100.00 |
| DURATION | | | Num 8 | | . | SAS missing (.) | 501 | 100.00 | 501 | 100.00 |
| | | | | | to | Range | 0 | 0.00 | 501 | 100.00 |
| LANGUAGE | Language | | Num 8 | | . | SAS missing (.) | 501 | 100.00 | 501 | 100.00 |
| | | | | | to | Range | 0 | 0.00 | 501 | 100.00 |
| STATUS | | | Num 8 | 2.00 | . | SAS missing (.) | 0 | 0.00 | 0 | 0.00 |
| | | | | | 2 to 2 | Range | 501 | 100.00 | 501 | 100.00 |
| NUM_DOC_VISITS | Number of doctor visits in the past year | | Num 8 | 3.00 | . | SAS missing (.) | 0 | 0.00 | 0 | 0.00 |
| | | | | | 3 to 3 | Range | 501 | 100.00 | 501 | 100.00 |

## Understanding the Potential Problem Reports

For data sets with many variables, it can be very tedious to examine each variable to detect anomalies that need investigating. The %TK_codebook macro identifies several types of anomalies in the variables and summarizes them in the optional potential problem reports. These reports are printed following the codebook. As a member of the data preparation team, you will use these reports to identify and correct problems with the data. You will save time by reviewing these reports and correcting problems before examining the information printed on every variable listed in the codebook.

### Incomplete Format Report

This report lists formats that are missing values occurring in one or more variables to which they are assigned. The name of the FORMAT is listed in the first column of the report with the omitted value listed in the second column.

**Report 3-1: Incomplete Format Report**

| POTENTIAL PROBLEM: INCOMPLETE FORMAT Variable has value not in assigned FORMAT definition. Check FORMAT definitions. If correct, check OUT OF RANGE VALUE report. | | |
|---|---|---|
| **Format** | **Value not in Format** | **Number of Variables with Value** |
| HEALTH | 6 | 1 |
| WEIGHT | 0 | 1 |

To investigate this problem, check to see whether the value listed in the "Value not in Format" column was expected to occur for any variable that is assigned to the format. From Program 3-1 you can find out the format WEIGHT has the following five categories defined when it was created by PROC FORMAT:

   1 = Very underweight

   2 = Somewhat underweight

   3 = Healthy weight

   4 = Somewhat overweight

   5 = Very Overweight

Our report shows the value of zero (0) also occurs in the data set for at least one variable assigned to format WEIGHT. If a value of zero is valid for this format, then the PROC FORMAT code that creates the WEIGHT format in Program 3-1 should be modified to include the value. If zero is not a valid category, then look at the "Out of Range Value Report" to find the name of the variable(s) that have invalid values.

## Out of Range Value Report

Report 3-2 lists the names of variables having values that are missing from the assigned user-defined FORMAT. If you have determined that the format assigned to this variable does correctly identify all of the expected values, then your next step is to investigate, correct, recode, or document the out of range value in the variables identified in this report. If the value is invalid, then do the following to mitigate the problem:

- Determine whether the data collection system needs to be updated to prevent this value from being entered.

- Determine the correct value and update in the data. The correct value can sometimes be determined from other questions or variables, reviewing computer logs, or contacting the participant.

- If it is not possible to determine the correct value, then consider choosing from the following actions:

  ○ Let the out of range value appear as listed in the codebook

  ○ Modify the FORMAT to add the value and assign a unique value label

  ○ Recode value to missing.

**Report 3-2: Out of Range Value Report**

| POTENTIAL PROBLEM: OUT OF RANGE VALUE Variable has values not in FORMAT definition. Investigate out of range value if FORMAT is correct. | | | |
|---|---|---|---|
| **Variable Name** | **Label** | **Out of Range Value** | **Format** |
| HEALTH | How is your health | 6 | HEALTH |
| WEIGHT | How would you describe your weight | 0 | WEIGHT |

## No Variation in Response Report

Variables with no variation in response values need to be investigated in sample surveys. These variables might be system variables that are expected to have only one value, but research variables with no variation in response are uncommon. Report 3-3 lists all numeric variables that have only one value (other than missing). Below we see that the only response for the NUM_DOC_VISITS variable is a value of 3 and 100% of the participants gave this answer. The STATUS variable has a value of 2 for all participants. These variables should be examined to determine whether it is reasonable that there is no variation.

## Report 3-3: No Variation in Response Report

| Variable Name | Label | Frequency Category | Minimum | Maximum | Frequency | Percent |
|---|---|---|---|---|---|---|
| **POTENTIAL PROBLEM: NUMERIC VARIABLES WITH NO VARIATION IN RESPONSE** All nonmissing values are the same for these variables | | | | | | |
| NUM_DOC_VISITS | Number of doctor visits past year | Range | 3 | 3 | 501 | 100.00 |
| STATUS | | Range | 2 | 2 | 501 | 100.00 |

## Variables with No Assigned User Format

The next two tables list the character and numeric variables that do not have a user-defined format assigned. The table for character variables appears in Report 3-4.

## Report 3-4: Character Variables Not Assigned Report

| Variable Name | Type | Variable Length | Variable Label |
|---|---|---|---|
| **POTENTIAL PROBLEM: CHARACTER VARIABLES NOT ASSIGNED USER FORMAT** Codebook combines all values in the category 'BLANK, TEXT, OR VALUE SUPPLIED' Try format with categories 'BLANK', 'TEXT OR VALUE SUPPLIED' | | | |
| CITY | Char | 10 | Fictional city where participant lives |

For character variables that do not have a format assigned, the %TK_codebook macro will lump all observations into one category called "Blank, Text, or Value supplied". Consider assigning a format that will separate out the "Blank" responses from the responses that contain actual information by using a format such as the $anytext format shown below.

```
proc format;
value $anytext ' '='Missing (blank)' other='Text or value supplied';
run;
```

The table for numeric variables without an assigned user-defined format appears below. The %TK_codebook macro reports frequency and percent for the range of nonmissing values for each of these variables. The variables BIRTHDATE and INT_DATE are date variables and have been assigned the SAS format mmddyy10. rather than a user-defined format. Since %TK_codebook uses this format to display the range of dates in the codebook you do not need to assign a different format.

Report 3-5: Numeric Variables Not Assigned A User-Defined Format Report

| POTENTIAL PROBLEM: NUMERIC VARIABLES NOT ASSIGNED A USER-DEFINED FORMAT<br>Codebook uses categories 'Range', 'SAS Missing (.)'<br>Assign format with categories 'Valid Range', 'Missing'<br>Values outside of Valid Range will be identified in Out of Range Report. | | | |
|---|---|---|---|
| **Variable Name** | **Type** | **Variable Length** | **Variable Label** |
| AGE | Num | 8 | Age at interview date |
| BIRTHDATE | Num | 8 | Date of birth |
| CASEID | Num | 8 | Unique identifier for participant |
| DURATION | Num | 8 | |
| EXER_DAYS | Num | 8 | In the Past 30 days, how many days did you exercise at least 30 minutes? |
| INT_DATE | Num | 8 | Interview date |
| LANGUAGE | Num | 8 | Language |
| NUM_DOC_VISITS | Num | 8 | Number of doctor visits past year |
| SMOKE | Num | 8 | Do you currently smoke? |
| STATUS | Num | 8 | |

For numeric variables that represent amounts rather than categories , it is useful to assign a format to define the valid range. For example, the EXER_DAYS variable should always be 0 to 30 days. If special codes are assigned to document the reason missing, then the following format would be useful to assign to EXER_DAYS so that the codebook reports the actual number of valid responses, any out of range values, and the reason for missing. Out of range values are identified and reported in the "Out of Range Value" report.

```
proc format;
value DAYS -9 = "Don't Know" -8="Not Asked" -7="Refused" 0-30="Valid
Response";
run;
```

This table includes some variables such as SMOKE that have values representing categories and need a format assigned:

```
proc format;
value smoke 0="No" 1="Yes";
run;
```

## Undefined Variable Label Report

The final report printed lists the names of the variables that are missing a label or have a label that matches the name of the variable.

**Report 3-6: Undefined Variable Label Report**

| POTENTIAL PROBLEM: UNDEFINED VARIABLE LABEL Variable is missing label or has label matching variable name. | | |
|---|---|---|
| **Variable Name** | **Label** | **Potential Problem** |
| DURATION | | Missing variable label |
| LANGUAGE | Language | Label identical to variable name |
| STATUS | | Missing variable label |

# Inside the Toolkit: %TK_codebook

The %TK_codebook macro is actually a super PROC as it combines the output of PROC CONTENTS, PROC FORMAT, PROC MEANS, PROC FREQ, PROC REPORT, and PROC SORT with a few DATA steps to create a codebook. ODS is used to package this codebook nicely in your choice of formats. Rather than discussing the over 1200 lines of code that creates %TK_codebook, this section provides some useful tips to using %TK_codebook.

%TK_codebook will automatically add the ODS statements that you need to get your codebook formatted for the ODS destinations XML, XLSX, PDF, and RTF. The %TK_codebook program differs from all other macro programs that accompany this book with this feature.

Much of the power of %TK_codebook is that you use formats to communicate information about the values that are valid and enable you to customize how this information is presented to your user. Here are some tips to remember when you create your formats.

- Use formats to hide the values of sensitive data that should not be displayed to the public by assigning formats to the variables that report only two categories, Missing and Present.

- Use formats to define every valid value for a variable, or the range of valid values for a variable. This allows TK_codebook to identify all the out of range values as well as formats that might be missing a value definition.

%TK_codebook will return the data set it constructs to create your codebook. Example 4-3 in the "Customizing Codebooks" chapter presents the custom template used for ODS and a macro that uses PROC REPORT to produce the FULL codebook. These two programs can serve as a starting point for you to format your own codebook. Example 4-4 shows you how to add additional information such as:

- The complete question text for each variable or
- Skip pattern instructions for each variable to the codebook output data set.

Example 4-4 show you how to create a codebook with a very different design than the codebook created with %TK_codebook.

# Summary

This chapter illustrated using the %TK_codebook macro to create a codebook and reports that uncover potential problems with the data. A codebook is a critical step in the management of any data collection or analysis project. It is a reference for the project and analysis team, a rapid introduction to the data for new users, and serves as a communication tool for preparers, funding agency, primary research lead, and other investigators who want to use the data. Using title statements, assigning labels and formats to your variables with the %TK_codebook macro tool, you can create a comprehensive codebook that includes the following information:

- Background information
  - Who collected the data
  - Why the data was collected
  - How the data was collected
- Technical Information
  - Number of observations and variables in the data set
  - Date the data set was created
  - Organization of the data
- Sampling information that you add in title statements
  - Who or what is the unit of observation
  - How the units of observation were selected
  - What variables describe the sampling strategy
- Variable Information
  - Variable name
  - Variable label
  - Format assigned to the variable
  - Data type and length in bytes
  - Value codes, meaning, and distribution of responses for categorical or nominal variables
  - Descriptive statistics for numeric variables

The potential problem reports can be used as an aid in managing data quality during collection and uncover problems in data sets received from outside sources. They will also reduce the workload of programmers who are responsible for cleansing the data by automatically creating a list of variables with potential problems including the following:

- Incomplete formats
- Out of range values
- No variation in response values
- Variables not assigned a user-defined format
- Variables missing labels

The next chapter explores the %TK_codebook macro in detail and will teach you to customize your codebook. You will learn how to add text decorations to enhance titles in your codebook and how to use the output data set from %TK_codebook to personalize the codebook for your project.

# Chapter 4: Customizing Codebooks

## Introduction

The codebook that you learned to produce in the last chapter is a great way to get to know your data and easily detect mistakes and unexpected results. In this chapter you will learn to modify your codebook to suit the needs of your project. You will learn how to:

- Embellish titles

- Add a logo to your codebook

- Obtain an output data set with all the variables needed to design your own codebook

- Overcome the 256-character limit imposed by using the label of your variable as its description in the codebook

- Customize the technical information and appearance of the table describing the variables in your codebook

These examples illustrate some easy ways to use features in SAS to customize your codebook.

## Example 4-1: Embellishing Titles

An easy way to embellish titles is by using options that control the appearance of text in the TITLE or FOOTNOTE statements for ODS destinations such as HTML, RTF, PDF, and EXCEL. You can even select unique formatting for different parts of your title as shown in the general form of the TITLE and FOOTNOTE statements shown below:

```
TITLE options 'text-1' options 'text-2' . . . options 'text-n';
FOOTNOTE options 'text-1' options 'text-2'  . . . options 'text-n';
```

The following options shown in Table 4-1 can be used in these statements to embellish your titles.

**Table 4-1: Options for Embellishing Titles and Footnotes**

| Action | Option | Destination |
|---|---|---|
| Specify text color | COLOR= | ODS HTML, RTF, PRINTER |
| Specify background color for the text | BCOLOR= | ODS HTML, RTF, PRINTER |
| Specify font for text | FONT= | ODS HTML, RTF, PRINTER |
| Make text bold | BOLD | ODS HTML, RTF, PRINTER |
| Make text italic | ITALIC | ODS HTML, RTF, PRINTER |
| Specify height of the text | HEIGHT= | |
| Justify text Left, Right, or Center | JUSTIFY= | |
| Underline subsequent text (0 indicates no underlining, ODS prints same line weight for values 1,2,3) | UNDERLIN=0\|1\|2\|3 | ODS HTML, RTF, PRINTER |

Program 4-1 uses these options to add a background color, change height, and add bold or italic to the formatting of titles when creating a codebook. This program is divided into five sections.

*Section 1:* This section creates titles used in the codebook. The first title serves as the main title for our codebook. It is centered with a height of 14 point and printed using bold, italicized Arial font with a background color of light gray. The footnote is left-justified and printed with a height of 9 point in the default font defined by the template used to create the codebook. All titles and footnotes that you define will be printed on every page of the codebook.

*Section 2:* This section defines names and folders and includes the %TK_codebook macro.

The first three statements create SAS macro variables that store names of folders used in the program. The LIBNAME statement that follows associates the library reference SAS_data with the folder containing data that we need to access.

The FMTSEARCH= system option on the next line tells SAS to include searching for format definitions in a catalog named FORMATS.sas7bcat in the folder defined by the libref SAS_data.

SAS will first search the temporary format catalog WORK.FORMATS, and then search the LIBRARY.FORMATS catalog before searching catalogs listed in the FMTSEARCH= system option.

The last two statements set up the programming information that will be used to create the codebook. The full pathname of the codebook that we are producing is defined by macro variable &CB_NAME created by the %LET statement. The %INCLUDE statement reads in the SAS statements for the %TK_codebook macro program and includes processing information as part of the SAS job. To see the source code created by the SAS macro processor for the %INCLUDE statements that you can add the SOURCE2 and MPRINT options to the OPTIONS statement in your SAS program:

```
options source2 mprint;
```

*Section 3:* The DATA step in this section asks SAS to create a data set using only 5 variables in the data set. A label is added to this data set providing more information about the data set. The RETAIN statement appears before the SET statement to define the internal ordering of the variables in the data set. The $showall. format is defined in the format catalog created in Chapter 3 and will ask the %TK_codebook macro to show all the formatted values of the variable CITY in the codebook.

*Section 4:* The last section in the program invokes the %TK_codebook macro program. The keyword parameter specifications request the %TK_codebook macro to use the data set created in the previous section and the format catalog (formats.sas7bcat) located in the folder associated with the SAS libref SAS_data. The %TK_codebook macro will only search this folder to find the formats that will be used in creating the codebook.

The codebook is created with the RTF type and saved in a file with the full pathname assigned to the &cb_name variable in Section 2. This allows the codebook to be opened with Microsoft Word. The variables are listed in the internal order (the order they occur in the data set) and the FORMAT assigned to each variable and the mean value columns are omitted from the listing since we chose to create a BRIEF codebook.

### Program 4-1: Embellish Titles

```
options papersize=letter orientation=portrait leftmargin=1.5in
rightmargin=1.5in topmargin=1.5in bottommargin=1.5in;
options nodate nonumber;

* Section 1) Add options to embellish titles and footnotes;
title j=center height=14pt font=Arial Bold Italic  bcolor="LTGRAY"
     "Master Codebook for Study A Health Data";
footnote j=left height=9pt
     "Data created for illustrating the Data Detective's Toolkit.";

* Section 2) Define folders, name of codebook, and include codebook
program;
%let TKFolder = /Data_Detective/Book/SAS_programs/TK_toolkit;
%let DataFolder = /Data_Detective/Book/SAS_Data sets;
%let WorkFolder = /Data_Detective/Book/SAS_Output;
libname SAS_data "&DataFolder";
options fmtsearch = (SAS_data.formats);
%let cb_name=&WorkFolder/Codebook4_1.rtf;
```

```
%include "&TKFolder/TK_codebook.sas";

* Section 3) Get data, make modifications as needed;
data StudyA(label="Health Data Simulated as a Simple Random Sample for
Participants in Study A");
      retain caseid city race sex birthdate;
      set SAS_data.StudyA(keep = caseid birthdate sex race city);
      format city $showall.;
run;

* Section 4) Create codebook;
%TK_codebook(lib=work,
      file1=StudyA,
      fmtlib=SAS_data,
      cb_type=RTF,
      cb_file=&cb_name,
      var_order=internal,
      cb_size=BRIEF,
      organization = One record per Participant (CASEID),
      include_warn=NO);
run;
```

The codebook created with these statements appears in Codebook 4-1. The appearance of the main title has been enhanced by the options that we included in the TITLE statement.

## Codebook 4-1: Codebook Created Using Options in TITLE and FOOTNOTE Statements

### *Master Codebook for Study A Health Data*

*Data Set: StudyA.sas7bdat*
*Label: Health Data Simulated as a Simple Random Sample for Participants in Study A*
*Date Created: 13JUL20:17:10:06*
*Number of Observations: 501     Number of Variables: 5*
*Organization of Data Set: One record per Participant (CASEID)*

| Variable Name | Label | Type | Values | Frequency Category | Frequency | Percent |
|---|---|---|---|---|---|---|
| CASEID | Unique identifier for participant | Num 8 | . | SAS missing (.) | 0 | 0.00 |
| | | | 10000 to 10500 | Range | 501 | 100.00 |
| CITY | Fictional city where participant lives | Char 20 | Emerald Falls | Emerald Falls | 179 | 35.73 |
| | | | Garnetville | Garnetville | 83 | 16.57 |
| | | | New Diamond | New Diamond | 141 | 28.14 |

| | | | | Ruby | Ruby | 98 | 19.56 |
|---|---|---|---|---|---|---|---|
| RACE | Race/Ethnicity | Num 8 | . | | SAS Missing (.) | 30 | 5.99 |
| | | | 1 | | White | 270 | 53.89 |
| | | | 2 | | Hispanic | 47 | 9.38 |
| | | | 3 | | Black | 130 | 25.95 |
| | | | 4 | | Asian | 24 | 4.79 |
| SEX | Sex of participant | Num 8 | 1 | | Male | 249 | 49.70 |
| | | | 2 | | Female | 252 | 50.30 |
| BIRTHDATE | Date of birth | Num 8 | . | | SAS missing (.) | 45 | 8.98 |
| | | | 05/28/1967 to 03/30/1992 | | Range | 456 | 91.02 |

*Data created for illustrating the Data Detective's Toolkit*

# Example 4-2: Add a Logo to Your Codebook

SAS enables you to insert an image or logo in your document using either TITLE statements or PROC TEMPLATE. The logo or image that you want to insert needs to be formatted as a JPG, PNG, GIF, BMP, or TIFF file. The SAS code from the previous example was modified to add a logo at the top of a codebook and is shown in Program 4-2.

*Section 1:* The statements in Section 1 of the SAS program from the previous example were changed to allow SAS to use inline formatting to insert the image. First, an escape character was defined with the ODS ESCAPECHAR= command to allow SAS to identify the portion of the character string appearing in the TITLE statement that should be interpreted as a formatting symbol. The character that you choose should be one that is rarely used, such as ^ or @.

The TITLE1 statement instructs SAS to center the image (J=CENTER) and the "^S" that follows tells SAS where the logo imported from the file "HealthWatch2020_v2.jpg" should be placed. A second title was added to be centered under the logo.

*Section 2:* The name of the codebook was changed in the %LET CB_NAME statement to differ from the previous example. No additional changes were needed in the remainder of the code from Program 4-1.

### Program 4-2: Add Logo to Codebook

```
options papersize=letter orientation=portrait leftmargin=1.5in
rightmargin=1.5in topmargin=1.5in bottommargin=1.5in;
options nodate nonumber;
```

```
* Section 1) Add options to embellish titles and footnotes;
ods escapechar='^';
title1 j=center '^S={preimage= "/Data_Detective/Book/SAS_Data
sets/HealthWatch2020_v2.jpg"}';
title2 j=center height=14pt Bold Italic  "Master Codebook for Study A
Health Data";
footnote j=left height=9pt "Data Created for Illustrating the Data
Detective's Toolkit";

* Section 2) Define folders, name of codebook, and include codebook
program.;
%let TKFolder = /Data_Detective/Book/SAS_programs/TK_toolkit;
%let DataFolder = /Data_Detective/Book/SAS_Data sets;
%let WorkFolder = /Data_Detective/Book/SAS_Output;
libname SAS_data "&DataFolder";
options fmtsearch = (SAS_data.formats);
%let cb_name=&WorkFolder/Codebook4_2.rtf;

%include "&TKFolder/TK_codebook.sas";

* Section 3) Get data, make modifications as needed;
data StudyA(label="Data Simulated as a Simple Random Sample for
Participants in Study A");
      set SAS_data.StudyA(keep = caseid birthdate sex race city);
      format city $showall.;
run;

* Section 4) Create codebook;
%TK_codebook(lib=work,
      file1=StudyA,
      fmtlib=SAS_data,
      cb_type=RTF,
      cb_file=&cb_name,
      var_order=internal,
      cb_size=BRIEF,
      organization = One record per Participant (CASEID),
      include_warn=NO);
run;
```

The output created with Program 4-2 is shown in Codebook 4-2. The logo now appears centered in the header, followed by the main title used in the previous example.

Codebook 4-2: Codebook with Logo Inserted in Title

# 🜨 🜂 Health Watch 2020 🜍 📖

## *Master Codebook for Study A Health Data*

*Data Set:  StudyA.sas7bdat*
*Label:  Data Simulated as a Simple Random Sample for Participants in Study A*
*Date Created:  13JUL20:17:42:39*
*Number of Observations:  501     Number of Variables:  5*
*Organization of Data Set:  One record per Participant (CASEID)*

| Variable Name | Label | Type | Values | Frequency Category | Frequency | Percent |
|---|---|---|---|---|---|---|
| CITY | Fictional city where participant lives | Char 20 | Emerald Falls | Emerald Falls | 179 | 35.73 |
| | | | Garnetville | Garnetville | 83 | 16.57 |
| | | | New Diamond | New Diamond | 141 | 28.14 |
| | | | Ruby | Ruby | 98 | 19.56 |
| CASEID | Unique identifier for participant | Num 8 | . | SAS missing (.) | 0 | 0.00 |
| | | | 10000 to 10500 | Range | 501 | 100.00 |
| BIRTHDATE | Date of birth | Num 8 | | SAS missing (.) | 45 | 8.98 |
| | | | 05/28/1967 to 03/30/1992 | Range | 456 | 91.02 |
| SEX | Sex of participant | Num 8 | 1 | Male | 249 | 49.70 |
| | | | 2 | Female | 252 | 50.30 |
| RACE | Race/Ethnicity | Num 8 | . | SAS Missing (.) | 30 | 5.99 |
| | | | 1 | White | 270 | 53.89 |
| | | | 2 | Hispanic | 47 | 9.38 |
| | | | 3 | Black | 130 | 25.95 |
| | | | 4 | Asian | 24 | 4.79 |

# Example 4-3: Codebook Output Data Set and Default Design

This example illustrates how to get an output data set with all of the variables needed to print a codebook. You will also learn how the template and SAS code used by the %TK_codebook macro work to format the codebook. This provides a blueprint for using the output data set to create codebooks with a different design than what you get from the %TK_codebook macro. Here is the strategy that you can use to customize your codebook:

1. Run the %TK_codebook macro and get an output data set containing the variables created for the codebook
2. Augment the data set as needed
   a. Merge additional codebook variables with new information about each variable in the original data set

   b.  Combine existing codebook variables
   c.  Change labels of the codebook variables
3.  Identify or create a style sheet to format the codebook
4.  Print codebook

Program 4-3 follows this strategy to use an output data set from the %TK_codebook macro along with ODS, a custom template, and PROC REPORT to create a codebook identical to one you would obtain from %TK_codebook.

**Program 4-3: Using an Output Data Set to Create a Codebook**

```
/* Section 1) Add options to embellish titles and footnotes;*/
ods escapechar='^';
title1 j=center '^S={preimage="/Data_Detective/Book/SAS_Data
sets/HealthWatch2020_v2.jpg"}';
title2 j=center height=14pt Bold Italic  "Master Codebook for Study A
Health Data";
footnote j=left height=9pt "Data Created for Illustrating the Data
Detective's Toolkit";

/* Section 2) Define folders, name of codebook, and include codebook
program.; */
%let TKFolder = /Data_Detective/Book/SAS_programs/TK_toolkit;
%let DataFolder = /Data_Detective/Book/SAS_Data sets;
%let WorkFolder = /Data_Detective/Book/SAS_Output;
libname SAS_data "&DataFolder";
options fmtsearch = (SAS_data.formats);
%let cb_name=&WorkFolder/Codebook4_3.rtf;

%include "&TKFolder/TK_codebook.sas";

/* Section 3) Get data, make modifications as needed; */
data StudyA(label="Data Simulated as a Simple Random Sample for
Participants in Study A");
     set SAS_data.StudyA(keep = caseid birthdate sex race city);
     format city $showall.;
run;

/* Section 4) Run the TK_codebook macro and get an output data set; */
%TK_codebook(lib=work,
     file1=StudyA,
     fmtlib=SAS_data,
     var_order=internal,
     /*
     cb_type=RTF,
     cb_file=&cb_name,
     cb_size=BRIEF,
     include_warn=NO,
     organization = One record per Participant (CASEID),
     */
     cb_output=CB_data);
run;
```

```
* Examine variables from the data set containing all variables needed to
print the codebook;
proc contents data=CB_data varnum;
run;

/* Section 5) Optionally use a DATA step to modify CB_data to create
additional variables, change labels, etc. */
* No changes made to CB_data;
/* Section 6) Create Codebook matching a FULL codebook created by
TK_codebook.sas macro; */
%let ProgramFolder = /Data_Detective/Book/SAS_programs/Ch4_examples;

/* Section 6a) Set up formatting instructions for codebook. */
* Set default margins;
options papersize=letter orientation=landscape leftmargin=1.5in
rightmargin=1.5in topmargin=1.5in bottommargin=1.5in;

* Include Style sheet to define formatting for RTF file;
%include "&ProgramFolder/Prog4_4_template.sas";

/* Section 6b) Run the SAS program that prints the codebook and saves in
an RTF file; */
* Optional: include the organization of the data set used to create the
output data set (CB_data). If defined this will be listed in;
* the information block appearing before the codebook.;
%let organization = One record per Participant (CASEID);

%include "&ProgramFolder/Prog4_5_cb_report.sas";
ods rtf file="&cb_name" style=CB_design;

%PrintCodebook_full(my_codebook_data=CB_data);
ods rtf close;
run;
```

*Section 1 to 3:* Note that except for updating the name of the codebook in the macro variable &cb_name in Section 2 of Program 4-3, the SAS statements in Sections 1, 2, and 3 are identical to the Program 4-2 used in the previous example.

*Section 4:* Five of the TK_codebook parameter definitions for creating the codebook in the previous example have been commented out and a parameter definition (cb_output = ) added to get an output data set named CB_data that has all of the constructed variables needed for printing the codebook. Although no document will be created for the codebook, the codebook itself and the potential problem reports are printed in the Results window. Warning messages for the potential problems are also printed in the log file. Leaving the commented statements in would have created Codebook4_3.rtf in addition to providing an output data set named CB_data.

The variable list from the PROC CONTENTS output (Table 4-2) describes the 19 variables in the output data set (CB_data) created to capture the codebook information needed for the STUDYA data set. There is one row per NAME*DESC (unique Frequency Category for a variable) in the data set. The first five variables are used to create the first four lines of descriptive information appearing after the title of the default FULL codebook. Eleven of the remaining variables are the columns appearing in the variable information table in the codebook that describes the variables in STUDYA. The remaining three variables are used to correctly order each row printed in the codebook.

**Table 4-2: Variables in the Output Data Set Obtained from %TK_codebook**

| # | Variable | Type | Len | Format | Label |
|---|----------|------|-----|--------|-------|
| 1 | set_name | Char | 15 | | Data set name |
| 2 | set_label | Char | 70 | | Data set label |
| 3 | date_created | Char | 16 | | Date data set created |
| 4 | num_obs | Char | 3 | | Number of observations in data set |
| 5 | num_var | Char | 1 | | Number of variables in data set |
| 6 | order | Num | 8 | | Variable number order |
| 7 | name | Char | 32 | | Variable name |
| 8 | label | Char | 256 | | Variable label |
| 9 | format | Char | 32 | | Variable format |
| 10 | type_length | Char | 9 | | Variable type and length |
| 11 | mean_char | Char | 15 | | Mean of values for numeric variable |
| 12 | order_flag | Num | 8 | | Requested order of variables and values (RANGE/DESC) categories |
| 13 | range | Char | 40 | | Code or Value |
| 14 | cnt | Num | 8 | | Order of value defined by RANGE and DESC as it would appear in PROC FREQ output |
| 15 | desc | Char | 37 | | Value description |

| # | Variable | Type | Len | Format | Label |
|---|----------|------|-----|--------|-------|
| 16 | frequency | Num | 8 | BEST8. | Frequency |
| 17 | percent | Num | 8 | 6.2 | Percent |
| 18 | CumFrequency | Num | 8 | BEST8. | Cumulative frequency |
| 19 | CumPercent | Num | 8 | 6.2 | Cumulative percent |

*Section 5:* At this point in your SAS program, you can modify the output data set from %TK_codebook. No modifications are made to the data set for this example. Example 4-4 illustrates modifications to this output data set to tailor the codebook to your project.

*Section 6:* After making any adjustments to the output data set CB_data, you now have complete flexibility to design the codebook that you need for your project. The first statement (%let ProgramFolder) creates a macro variable for the folder where the SAS programs that need to be included as part of this job are located. Although the remaining SAS code in this program creates the same format of the codebook as the %TK_codebook macro produces, you will be able to use the two macro programs that are included (%INCLUDE statements) in Section 6 and 6a of the SAS job stream as a guideline for your own design.

*Section 6a:* Much of the appearance of your code book is shaped by the options statement and the style sheet used to define the formatting for the ODS destination of your choice. A special style sheet created using PROC TEMPLATE (shown in Program 4-4) is included in the SAS job stream by using the following statement:

```
%include "&ProgramFolder/Prog4_4_template.sas";
```

This program creates a template that defines the font type and size and appearances of tables. The details of this SAS code shown in Program 4-4 will be discussed following the output displayed in Codebook 4-3.

*Section 6b:* This section has SAS statements to print your codebook. The first statement (%let organization =) in this section creates a macro variable defining the organization of your SAS data set (StudyA) used to create the output data set CB_data containing the codebook data. The organization identifies the "unit of observation" in your data set. The unit of observation is one or more variables that uniquely identifies the object (or person) about which (or who) collected information is stored in one record. For example, you might be taking repeated measurements on the same people at different interviews conducted biannually. In this instance, the organization of your data could be described by PERSON_ID*INTERVIEW. If defined, the macro variable defined by the "%let organization =" statement will be included in the descriptive information printed at the beginning of your codebook.

The actual printing of the codebook is handled by PROC REPORT in the macro included in the SAS job stream by the next four statements:

```
%include "&ProgramFolder/Prog4_5_cb_report.sas";
ods rtf file="&cb_name" style=CB_design;

%PrintCodebook_full(my_codebook_data=CB_data);
ods rtf close;
```

After including the SAS statements from Program4-3b_cb_report.sas as part of the job stream, ODS is used to open a file using the style sheet named CB_design created in Section 6a for the codebook. The PrintCodebook_full macro program uses the ODS text statement to print the descriptive information appearing after the title of the codebook and PROC REPORT to format the table displaying the variable information in the codebook. The details of this SAS code shown in both Program 4-4 (create template for printing codebook) and Program 4-5 (creating the formatted codebook) will be discussed following the output displayed in Codebook 4-3.

As you can see from Codebook 4-3, wrapping of column headers, variable names and other information occurs when the actual space you have to display the information about each variable is limited. Example 4-4 will show you how to create a custom design for your codebook to avoid this problem.

**Codebook 4-3: Codebook Created Using an Ouput Data Set from the %TK_codebook Macro**

# ⚕ 🧍 Health Watch 2020 🏃 📖

## *Master Codebook* for *Study A Health Data*

*Data Set: StudyA.sas7bdat*
*Label: Data Simulated as a Simple Random Sample for Participants in Study A*
*Date Created: 14JUL20:11:44:13*
*Number of Observations: 501      Number of Variables: 5*
*Organization of Data Set: One record per Participant (CASEID)*

| Variable name | Label | Format | Type | Mean | Values | Frequency Category | Frequency | Percent | Cumulative Frequency | Cumulative Percent |
|---|---|---|---|---|---|---|---|---|---|---|
| CITY | Fictional city where participant lives | $SHOWALL | Char 20 | | Emerald Falls | Emerald Falls | 179 | 35.73 | 179 | 35.73 |
| | | | | | Garnetvi lle | Garnetvi lle | 83 | 16.57 | 262 | 52.30 |
| | | | | | New Diamon d | New Diamon d | 141 | 28.14 | 403 | 80.44 |

| | | | | | | | | | | |
|---|---|---|---|---|---|---|---|---|---|---|
| | | | | | | Ruby | Ruby | 98 | 19.56 | 501 | 100.00 |

| | | | | | | | | | | |
|---|---|---|---|---|---|---|---|---|---|---|
| CASEID | Unique identifier for participant | | Num 8 | 10250 | . | SAS missing (.) | 0 | 0.00 | 0 | 0.00 |
| | | | | 10000 to 10500 | Range | 501 | 100.00 | 501 | 100.00 |

| | | | | | | | | | | |
|---|---|---|---|---|---|---|---|---|---|---|
| BIRTH DATE | Date of birth | MMDDYY1 0.0 | Num 8 | 07/15/1 979 | . | SAS missing (.) | 45 | 8.98 | 45 | 8.98 |
| | | | | 05/28/19 67 to 03/30/19 92 | Range | 456 | 91.02 | 501 | 100.00 |

| | | | | | | | | | | |
|---|---|---|---|---|---|---|---|---|---|---|
| SEX | Sex of participant | SEX | Num 8 | 1.50 | 1 | Male | 249 | 49.70 | 249 | 49.70 |
| | | | | | 2 | Female | 252 | 50.30 | 501 | 100.00 |

| | | | | | | | | | | |
|---|---|---|---|---|---|---|---|---|---|---|
| RACE | Race/Ethnici ty | RACE | Num 8 | 1.80 | . | SAS Missing (.) | 30 | 5.99 | 30 | 5.99 |
| | | | | | 1 | White | 270 | 53.89 | 300 | 59.88 |
| | | | | | 2 | Hispanic | 47 | 9.38 | 347 | 69.26 |
| | | | | | 3 | Black | 130 | 25.95 | 477 | 95.21 |
| | | | | | 4 | Asian | 24 | 4.79 | 501 | 100.00 |

*Data Created for Illustrating the Data Detective's Toolkit*

## Understanding the Default Codebook Template

The %TK_codebook macro takes advantage of the Output Delivery System (ODS) to format the printed codebook by creating a style template used to customize fonts, colors and borders in your document. Style templates can be created with the PROC TEMPLATE procedure. The easiest way to create your own template is to start with one of the style templates provided by SAS, and redefine certain sections of the code to design the codebook that you want. It is easy to get the SAS code for any of the templates printed in the SAS log file by running the following statements:

```
proc template;
source styles.template_name;
run;
```

Program 4-4 shows SAS statements to create a style template producing a codebook as if formatted created with the %TK_codebook macro. The first two statements in Program 4-4 use PROC TEMPLATE to create a new style template named CB_DESIGN. The third statement instructs SAS to base the new style CB_DESIGN on the parent style named RTF, but modify existing attributes of the RTF style with the SAS code that follows. The remaining SAS code uses the "class" syntax to overwrite the existing definitions of four style elements when creating the CB_DESIGN template. Any style elements or attributes in the parent style RTF not changed in this SAS code will be inherited from the RTF style element.

*Class Fonts:* The Font style element specifies the name of the font, font size, and the font weight for text used at different places in the ODS document that you are creating.

*Class Body from Document:* This style element defines the page margins of the ODS document that you are creating. This code specifies narrow margins of only .25 inch borders.

*Class Color List:* The Color List style element defines the colors and highlighting for your document. We will have black text and white background colors for the row and column headings as well as the page.

*Table from Output:* This style element defines the appearance of printed tables in your document by controlling the borders, placement of data within table cells, width of borders, and width of space between table cells.

**Program 4-4: Style template Used by %TK_codebook**

```
proc template;
   define style Styles.cb_design;
      parent=Styles.rtf;
      class fonts /
         'TitleFont' = ("Times",8pt,Bold Italic) /* Title statements */
         'TitleFont2' = ("Times",8pt,Bold Italic) /* Procedure Titles */
         'headingFont' = ("Times",8pt,Bold) /* Table column, row headings
*/
         'docFont' = ("Times",8pt)   /* Entries in table cells */
         'footFont' = ("Times",8pt);  /* Footnotes */
      class Body from Document /
         bottommargin = 0.25in
         topmargin = 0.25in
         rightmargin = 0.25in
         leftmargin = 0.25in;
      class color_list /
         'link' = blue
         'bgH' = white    /* Row and Column Headers */
         'fg' = black   /* Foreground Color for text */
         'bg' = white;   /* Page Background color */
      class Table from Output/
         frame=hsides  /* Outside Borders */
```

```
        rules=groups /* Internal Borders: none all, cols, rows, groups */
        cellpadding=3pt  /* Space between table cell contents and border */
        cellspacing=0pt  /* Space between table cells - background shows */
        borderwidth=.75pt; /* Width of borders and rules */
    end;
run;
```

## Formatting Your Codebook with the Default Codebook Design

The macro %PrintCodebook_Full shown in Program 4-5 uses the output data set from the %TK_codebook macro to print the formatted codebook.

*Section 1:* The first task of this macro program is to transfer the value of variables containing the data set name, label, date created, number of observations, and number of variables to macro variables. This is done using the CALL SYMPUTX routine to create a macro variable. The first argument enclosed in quotation marks is the name of the macro variable being created. The second argument is the value assigned to the macro variable. For this program the values come from a SAS variable, but they could also be a character constant or an expression.

*Section 2:* The second task of the %PrintCodebook_Full macro program is to create the data information block that appears at the beginning of the codebook. This is done with the ODS ESCAPECHAR and ODS TEXT statements. The ODS ESCAPECHAR statement enables you to insert control characters that indicate special formatting used to print the document. For this program, anytime ODS finds a caret (^) in the SAS code, it interprets what follows as a special sequence of characters instructing ODS how to create the output file. Here it is used to specify style characteristics for the text to be printed by using the following syntax:

```
ODS text = "^S={attribute1=value1 attribute2=value2 } text";
```

The attributes include font, font weight, font style, font size, justify, and color for customizing the text printed in the data information block.

One blank line inserted between the data information block and the variable table is added with this statement:

```
ods text = " ^{newline 1}";
```

*Section 3:* The last task in this macro is to use PROC REPORT to design the layout of the codebook variable table. Options in the PROC REPORT statement control the appearance of the header row showing column titles (style(header)= ) and the thin gray line separating rows in the variable table (style(summary)= ). Other design specifications used for formatting the variable table include the following:

- Left-justifies the report (nocenter)
- For ODS non-Listing destinations, prints data for columns on consecutive lines if the width of the report is not wide enough to display all columns (wrap)

- Splits the column heading if the specified character is found in the heading and continues heading on the next line (split='character')

- Consider missing values as valid values for group, order, across variables (missing)

The COLUMN statement controls the order of the columns. The DEFINE statement specifies how the values in each cell are formatted. Note that each column that is printed has a width specified as a percentage of the page width. These add up to less than 99% to ensure that all columns fit the width of the page without wrapping.

A separate label statement is used to define a shortened label for some columns.

**Program 4-5: SAS Statements to Create Codebook**

```
%macro PrintCodebook_Full (my_codebook_data=);
    /* SECTION 1) CREATE MACRO VARIABLES STORING DATA SET INFORMATION
       NEEDED FOR PRINTING CODEBOOK INFORMATION */
    data _null_;
        set &my_codebook_data(obs=1);
        call symputx('set_name', set_name);
        call symputx('set_label',set_label);
        call symputx('set_date',date_created);
        call symputx('obs_count',num_obs);
        call symputx('var_count',num_var);
    run;

    /* SECTION 2) PRINT INFORMATION BLOCK ABOUT DATA */

    ods escapechar='^';
    ods text = "^S={fontweight=bold fontstyle=italic} Data Set:
&set_name";
    ods text = "^S={fontweight=bold fontstyle=italic} Label:  &set_label
";
    ods text = "^S={fontweight=bold fontstyle=italic} Date Created:
&set_date";
    ods text = "^S={fontweight=bold fontstyle=italic} Number of
Observations:  &obs_count      Number of Variables:  &var_count";

    %if "&organization" ^= "" %then
        %do;
            ods text = "^S={fontweight=bold fontstyle=italic} Organization
of Data Set:  &organization";
        %end;

    ods text = " ^{newline 1}";

    /* SECTION 3) PRINT CODEBOOK */
    proc report data=&my_codebook_data nocenter wrap split='~'  missing
        style(header)=[color=black backgroundcolor=very light gray ]
        style(summary)=[color=very light gray backgroundcolor=very light
gray fontfamily="Times Roman" fontsize=1pt textalign=r];;
        /* Code for cb_size=FULL*/
        column order name label format type_length mean_char order_flag
range cnt desc frequency percent CumFrequency CumPercent;
        define order / group noprint;
        define name /group style(column)=[width=10%];
        define label /group flow style(column)=[width=16%];
```

```
      define type_length / group center style(column)=[width=5.0%];
      define mean_char / group center style(column)=[width=5.8%];
      define order_flag/ order noprint;
      define range / group flow center style(column)=[width=8.0%]
style(column)={tagattr="format:@"};
      define format /group style(column)=[width=6.5%];
      define cnt / order noprint;
      define desc  / group center flow  style(column)=[width=10.5%]
style(column)={tagattr="format:@"};
      define frequency / analysis style(column)=[width=7.8%]
format=comma10.0;
      define percent / analysis style(column)=[width=6.6%];
      define CumFrequency / analysis style(column)=[width=8.5%]
format=comma10.0;
      define CumPercent / analysis style(column)=[width=8.5%];
      label label="Label";
      label format="Format";
      label type_length = "Type";
      label mean_char = "Mean";
      label range = "Values";
      label desc = "Frequency Category";
      label CumFrequency = "Cumulative Frequency";
      label CumPercent = "Cumulative Percent";
      break after name  /suppress skip;
      break after name  /summarize suppress;
   run;

%mend;
```

# Example 4-4: Create a Custom Design for Your Codebook

In this example, you will create a custom design for your codebook with the following features:

- Add text longer than 256 characters to replace the label assigned the codebook variables in the output data set from %TK_codebook

- Display a separate frequency table for each variable in your original data set

- Display a variable information block before the corresponding frequency table that includes:

  o Variable Name

  o Variable Label

  o Data Type

  o Assigned format

  o Question Text

The program to create this new design is shown in Program 4-6.

*Section 1:* These statements use options to define the height, font, and color for the titles and footnote used in the codebook.

*Section 2:* This section of code defines macro variables to store the names of folders and codebooks that we are creating, assigns a libref to two of the folders, and includes the codebook program as part of the SAS job.

*Section 3:* The DATA step in this section reads in the data, keeps five of the variables and uses a RETAIN statement to order the variables in the new data set (work.StudyA). Using the RETAIN statement before the SET statement tells SAS to store the variables in the order they are listed on the RETAIN statement. This allows you to use the VAR_ORDER=INTERNAL option to easily control the order your variables are listed in your codebook created with %TK_codebook.

*Section 4:* An output data set is requested from %TK_codebook. Several parameters are omitted that we used in previous runs to get the codebook created in the standard format. We could have included these statements to have the standard codebook created. A PROC CONTENTS is run and the data printed. Since there are only 15 observations there is no need to restrict the number of observations printed.

*Section 5:* Some of the variables have longer text descriptions than can be stored in the label assigned to each variable. You might have these text descriptions stored in a file and read them into your SAS job. In this section, a data set (LONG_LABELS) is created with the long labels. Both the data set CB_DATA and LONG_LABELS are sorted by name. A DATA step merges the LONG_LABELS data set the CB_DATA. A new variable, VAR_NAME, is created by combining the name of the variable with the original SAS label.

**WARNING: You should sort the data set by variable ORDER_FLAG as done in the PROC SORT statement following the DATA step.** This establishes the correct ordering of records for printing. If you do not do this, then your codebook could possibly have the entries for each variable jumbled.

*Section 6:* You are ready to create the codebook. The statements in this section include the SAS code for the template used to format the custom codebook. A macro variable is used to define the organization of CB_data. This information was originally a parameter used by %TK_codebook to print the organization at the beginning of the codebook. Next, ODS is used for creating an RTF file for our codebook. The parameter sectionadata="\sbknone" tells SAS that any PROC run after the ODS text statements are printed should start in the same section as the ODS text statements. The bodytitle tells SAS that any TITLE statements should be written in the body of the report rather than in the header of the RTF document being created. A new SAS macro program (%PrintCodebook_2) is included with SAS statements for the custom design of the codebook. %PrintCodebook_2 runs next using the CB_data set as input.

**Program 4-6: Creating a Custom Codebook with an Output Data Set from %TK_codebook**

```
/* Section 1) Add options to embellish titles and footnotes;*/
title1 j=center height=14pt font=Arial Bold Italic
   color=black  "Health Watch 2020";
title2 j=center height=13pt font=Arial Bold Italic
   color=black  "Master Codebook for Study A Health Data";
footnote j=left height=9pt
   "Data Created for Illustrating the Data Detective's Toolkit";

/* Section 2) Define folders, name of codebook, and include codebook
program; */

%let TKFolder = /Data_Detective/Book/SAS_programs/TK_toolkit;
%let DataFolder = /Data_Detective/Book/SAS_Data sets;
%let WorkFolder = /Data_Detective/Book/SAS_Output;
libname SAS_data "&DataFolder";
libname Output "&WorkFolder";

options fmtsearch = (SAS_data.formats);
%let cb_name=&WorkFolder/Codebook4_4.rtf;

%include "&TKFolder/TK_codebook.sas";

/* Section 3) Get data, use retain statement to change order of variables
in data set; */
data StudyA(label="Data Simulated as a Simple Random Sample for
Participants in Study A");
retain caseid city sex race birthdate ;
   set SAS_data.StudyA(keep = caseid birthdate sex race city);
   format city $showall.;
run;

/* Section 4) Run the TK_codebook macro and get an output data set; */
%TK_codebook(lib=work,
   file1=StudyA,
   fmtlib=SAS_data,
   var_order=internal,
   cb_output=CB_data);
run;

* Examine variables from the data set containing all variables needed to
print the codebook;
proc contents data=CB_data varnum;
run;

proc print data=CB_data;
var order name order_flag range cnt desc CumPercent;
run;

/* Section 5) Use a DATA step to modify CB_data to create additional
variables, change labels, etc. */

* Longer, more informative labels for variables;

data long_labels;
   length name $ 32;
   length long_label $ 300;
```

```
   name = "CITY";
   long_label = "Fictional city where participant is located on date
interview is completed. (Note to analyst:  This might not be the city of
residence for the participant. No information is collected to determine
whether this location is the city of participant's permanent
residence.)";
   output;
   name = "RACE";
   long_label = 'Race/Ethnicity of participant. (Instructions to
participant:  "If you identify with multiple groups, please select the
one race or culture with whom you most closely identify.") ';
   output;
run;

proc sort data=long_labels; by name; run;

proc sort data=CB_data; by name; run;

data CB_data;
merge CB_data long_labels;
by name;
length var_name $360;
if missing(long_label) then long_label = label;
var_name =   compress(name) || " - " || strip(label) ;
run;

/* The next statement must be used to order the CB_data set correctly */
proc sort data=CB_data; by order_flag;
run;

proc print data=CB_data;
var name label long_label;
run;

/* Section 6) Create Codebook matching a FULL codebook created by
TK_codebook.sas macro; */
%let ProgramFolder = /Data_Detective/Book/SAS_programs/Ch4_examples;

/* Section 6a) Set up formatting instructions for codebook. */

* Include Style sheet to define formatting for RTF file;
%include "&ProgramFolder/Prog4_7_ND_template.sas";
run;
/* Section 6b) Run the SAS program that prints the codebook and saves in
an RTF file; */
* Optional: include the organization of the data set used to create the
output data set (CB_data). If defined this will be listed in;
* the information block appearing before the codebook.;
%let organization = One Record per Participant (CASEID);

%include "&ProgramFolder/Prog4_8_ND_cb_report.sas";

options orientation=portrait;
ods rtf file="&cb_name" style=CB2_design sectiondata="\sbknone"
bodytitle;
```

```
%PrintCodebook_2(my_codebook_data=CB_data);
ods rtf close;
run;
```

## Modifying the Default Codebook Template

The new template used to create the codebook is shown in Program 4-7. This is a slight modification from the template in Example 4-3. The SAS code for controlling the appearance of the BY line was added to this template. The BY line formats the appearance of the BY line that will be used in the new design of the codebook. To make the BY line stand out, the background is set to a light blue color with hexadecimal code (#BBDBF2) and the text will be written in bold print.

### Program 4-7: Template for New Design of Codebook

```
proc template;
define style Styles.CB2_design;
parent=Styles.RTF;
replace fonts /
'TitleFont' = ("Times Roman",12pt,Bold )
'TitleFont2' = ("Times Roman",12pt,Bold )
'ByFont' = ("Times Roman",12pt,Bold )
'StrongFont' = ("Times Roman",10pt,Bold)
'EmphasisFont' = ("Times Roman",10pt)
'headingEmphasisFont' = ("Times Roman",10pt,Bold )
'headingFont' = ("Times Roman",10pt,Bold)
'docFont' = ("Times Roman",10pt)
'footFont' = ("Times Roman",8pt)
'FixedEmphasisFont' = ("Times Roman",8pt)
'FixedStrongFont' = ("Times Roman",8pt,Bold)
'FixedHeadingFont' = ("Times Roman",8pt,Bold)
'BatchFixedFont' = ("Times Roman",6.7pt)
'FixedFont' = ("Times Roman",8pt);

*the next statement controls the appearance of the byline -- change
background color if needed;
class Byline from byline/
      color=black
      backgroundcolor = #BBDBF2
      font_weight=bold
      font_size = 11pt;
* the next statement controls appearance of the ods text statements;
style usertext from usertext/
      foreground=black
      fontsize=10pt
      fontstyle=roman
      fontweight=medium;

class Body from Document /
   bottommargin = 1.0in
   topmargin = 1.0in
   rightmargin = 1.0in
   leftmargin = 1.0in;
```

```
class color_list /
   'link' = blue  /*links */
   'bgH' = white  /*row and column header background*/
   'fg' = black   /*text color*/
   'bg' = white;  /* page background color */

class Table from Output/
   frame=hsides
   rules=groups /*all*/
   cellpadding=3pt
   cellspacing=0pt
   borderwidth=.75pt;
   end;
   run;
```

## Updating the Design of Your Codebook

The new design of the codebook will be created with the SAS code shown in Program 4-8.

*Section 1:* %TK_codebook created several macro variables having administrative and structural information about the STUDYA data set used by %TK_codebook to create CB_data. This includes the name and label of the STUDYA data set, creation date, number of observations, and number of variables. This information is stored in SAS macro variables with CALL SYMPUTX.

*Section 2:* ODS text statements are used to print the administrative and structural information at the beginning of the codebook. The ODS ESCAPCHAR= statement tells SAS that when it finds the character defined (^) the following text should be interpreted as formatting instructions for the ODS destination.

The ODS RTF STARTPAGE=NOW forces a page break. The ODS statements are used to print the administrative and structural information using the macro variables created in *Section 1*. After all the ODS statements are printed we use an ODS RTF STARTPAGE=NO to prevent a page break occurring before the PROC REPORT that follows.

*Section 3:* PROC REPORT is used to print the codebook. This is very similar to the PROC REPORT from Example 4-3. A BY statement has been added to get a separate frequency table printed for every variable (VAR_NAME) in the data set. A compute block has been added to get values of variables NAME, LABEL, TYPE_LENGTH, FORMAT, and LONG_LABEL printed before the frequency table.

**Program 4-8: SAS Statements for New Design of Codebook**

```
%macro PrintCodebook_2 (my_codebook_data=);
   /* SECTION 1) CREATE MACRO VARIABLES STORING DATA SET INFORMATION
NEEDED FOR PRINTING CODEBOOK INFORMATION */
   run;

   data _null_;
      set &my_codebook_data(obs=1);
      call symputx('set_name', set_name);
      call symputx('set_label', set_label);
      call symputx('set_date', date_created);
```

```
        call symputx('obs_count',num_obs);
        call symputx('var_count',num_var);
    run;

    /* SECTION 2) PRINT INFORMATION BLOCK ABOUT DATA */
    ods escapechar='^';
    ods rtf startpage=now;
    ods text = "^S={fontweight=bold fontstyle=italic just=l color=black
backgroundcolor=#BBDBF2 fontsize=12pt} Data Set Information" ;
    ods text= "^1n";
    ods text = "^S={fontweight=medium fontstyle=roman} Data Set:
&set_name";
    ods text = "^S={fontweight=medium fontstyle=roman} Label:  &set_label
";
    ods text = "^S={fontweight=medium fontstyle=roman} Date Created:
&set_date";
    ods text = "^S={fontweight=medium fontstyle=roman} Number of
Observations:  &obs_count";
    ods text = "^S={fontweight=medium fontstyle=roman} Number of
Variables:  &var_count";
    %if "&organization" ^= "" %then
        %do;
            ods text = "^S={fontweight=medium fontstyle=roman} Organization
of Data Set:  &organization";
        %end;
    title ' ';  /* omit title from appearing before PROC REPORT */
    ods text= "^2n";
    ods text = "^S={fontweight=bold fontstyle=italic just=l color=black
backgroundcolor=#BBDBF2 fontsize=12pt} Data Element Definitions" ;

    ods rtf startpage=no;

    /* Section 3) Print codebook */
proc report data=&my_codebook_data nowindows headline wrap
    split='~'  missing
    style(report) = [rules=all]
    style(header)=[color=black asis=on just=center
    bordertopcolor=black  background=#BBDBF2 borderrightcolor=black
    borderleftcolor=black bordertopwidth=.75pt]
    style(column)=[width=.7in]
    style(summary)=[color=very light blue backgroundcolor=blue
    fontfamily="Times Roman" fontsize=1pt textalign=l]
    style(lines)=[just=l asis=on bordertopcolor=white
    borderrightcolor=black borderleftcolor=black fontweight=medium
    borderbottomcolor=black
    listentrydblspace=no];
;
    column order  label var_name label long_label type_length format
    order name mean_char order_flag range cnt desc frequency percent
    CumFrequency CumPercent;

    define order / group noprint;
    define var_name / group noprint ;
    define label / group noprint;
    define long_label / group noprint;
    define type_length / group noprint;
    define format / group noprint;
    define name / group flow width=30 noprint;
```

```
   by var_name notsorted;

   break before var_name  / skip;
   break after var_name  / page /*skip*/;

   compute before _page_ ;
      line "Variable Name:    " name $50.;
      line "SAS Label:    " label $256.;
      line "Data Type:    " type_length $15.;
      line "SAS format:    " format $32.;
      line "   " ;
      line "Question Text:    " long_label $300.;
endcomp;

   define mean_char / group left  noprint ;
   define order_flag/ order noprint;
   define range / group flow left style=[cellwidth=1.0in]
      style(column)={tagattr="format:@"};
   define cnt / order noprint ;
   define desc  / group flow left style=[cellwidth=1.0in]
      style(column)={tagattr="format:@"};
   define frequency / analysis  left style=[cellwidth=0.6in]
      format=comma10.0 format=comma10.0
      style(column)={tagattr="format:@"};
   define percent / analysis  left style=[cellwidth=0.6in];
   define CumFrequency / analysis left style=[cellwidth=0.8in]
      format=comma10.0;
   define CumPercent / analysis left style=[cellwidth=0.8in];
   break after name  /suppress skip;
   label var_name = "Data Element";
   label frequency = "Count";
   label percent = "Percent";
   label desc = "Value Description";
   label CumFrequency = "Cumulative~Count";
   label CumPercent = "Cumulative~Percent";

run;
%mend;
```

The codebook with the new design is shown in Codebook 4-4.

**Codebook 4-4: New Design for Codebook Created with Output Data Set from %TK_codebook.**

## *Health Watch 2020*
## *Master Codebook for Study A Health Data*

### Data Set Information

Data Set:  StudyA.sas7bdat
Label:  Data Simulated as a Simple Random Sample for Participants in Study A
Date Created:  26AUG20:20:50:00
Number of Observations:  501

Number of Variables: 5
Organization of Data Set: One Record per Participant (CASEID)

## Data Element Definitions

### Data Element=CASEID - Unique identifier for participant

Variable Name: CASEID
SAS Label: Unique identifier for participant
Data Type: Num 8
SAS format:

Question Text: Unique identifier for participant

| Code or Value | Value Description | Count | Percent | Cumulative Count | Cumulative Percent |
|---|---|---|---|---|---|
| . | SAS missing (.) | 0 | 0.00 | 0 | 0.00 |
| 10000 to 10500 | Range | 501 | 100.00 | 501 | 100.00 |

### Data Element=CITY - Fictional city where participant lives

Variable Name: CITY
SAS Label: Fictional city where participant lives
Data Type: Char 20
SAS format: $SHOWALL

Question Text: Fictional city where participant is located on date interview is completed. (Note to analyst: This might not be the city of residence for the participant. No information is collected to determine whether this location is the city of participant's permanent residence.)

| Code or Value | Value Description | Count | Percent | Cumulative Count | Cumulative Percent |
|---|---|---|---|---|---|
| Emerald Falls | Emerald Falls | 179 | 35.73 | 179 | 35.73 |
| Garnetville | Garnetville | 83 | 16.57 | 262 | 52.30 |
| New Diamond | New Diamond | 141 | 28.14 | 403 | 80.44 |
| Ruby | Ruby | 98 | 19.56 | 501 | 100.00 |

## Data Element=SEX - Sex of participant

Variable Name:   SEX
SAS Label:   Sex of participant
Data Type:   Num 8
SAS format:  SEX

Question Text:   Sex of participant

| Code or Value | Value Description | Count | Percent | Cumulative Count | Cumulative Percent |
|---|---|---|---|---|---|
| 1 | Male | 249 | 49.70 | 249 | 49.70 |
| 2 | Female | 252 | 50.30 | 501 | 100.00 |

## Data Element=RACE - Race/Ethnicity

Variable Name:   RACE
SAS Label:   Race/Ethnicity
Data Type:   Num 8
SAS format:  RACE

Question Text:   Race/Ethnicity of participant. (Instructions to participant: "If you identify with multiple groups, please select the one race or culture with whom you most closely identify.")

| Code or Value | Value Description | Count | Percent | Cumulative Count | Cumulative Percent |
|---|---|---|---|---|---|
| . | SAS missing (.) | 30 | 5.99 | 30 | 5.99 |
| 1 | White | 270 | 53.89 | 300 | 59.88 |
| 2 | Hispanic | 47 | 9.38 | 347 | 69.26 |
| 3 | Black | 130 | 25.95 | 477 | 95.21 |
| 4 | Asian | 24 | 4.79 | 501 | 100.00 |

### Data Element=BIRTHDATE - Date of birth

Variable Name:    BIRTHDATE
SAS Label:    Date of birth
Data Type:    Num 8
SAS format:    MMDDYY10.0

Question Text:    Date of birth

| Code or Value | Value Description | Count | Percent | Cumulative Count | Cumulative Percent |
|---|---|---|---|---|---|
| . | SAS missing (.) | 45 | 8.98 | 45 | 8.98 |
| 05/28/1967 to 03/30/1992 | Range | 456 | 91.02 | 501 | 100.00 |

**Data Created for Illustrating the Data Detective's Toolkit**

# Summary

This chapter provides an introduction to ways that you can use SAS and ODS to customize your codebook. The ease of using the SAS ODS system to format reports will inspire you to tailor codebooks to meet the needs of your project and user community.

The easiest way to embellish your codebook is to simply add formatting and images to TITLE or FOOTNOTE statements, and then use the standard design from %TK_codebook to create your codebook. With the flexibility of obtaining an output data set from %TK_codebook, you can also design your own codebook layout, and then use a custom template and PROC REPORT (or other SAS PROC) to create your codebook.

# Chapter 5: Catalog Your Data

## Introduction

A project data catalog gives users a clear understanding of your data sets and helps answer the following questions:

- What do the variables in each data set represent?

- What do the values of each variable mean?

- What data is available for this project?

- Where is the data located?

- How are my data sets related to each other?

The codebook that you learned to create with the %TK_codebook macro is an important part of the data catalog and answers the first two questions. The *Data Detective's Toolkit* provides two additional macro programs to help you create documentation that answers the last three questions. The first macro data tool, %TK_inventory, will answer the third and forth questions by automatically creating a complete inventory of your SAS data sets in a given folder with descriptive details including number of observations, number of variables, creation date, and information stored in the label assigned to the data set. The second macro, %TK_xwalk, answers the last question by creating a crosswalk table showing equivalent variables common to a group of data sets. By consulting this table, you will uncover the variables linking data sets as well as help identify the location and relationship among all the variables needed for processing or analyzing your data.

# Using the %TK_inventory Macro

The %TK_inventory macro tool provides an easy way to create an inventory of all SAS data sets in a folder. This summary of all of your data is particularly useful for the following tasks:

- Reporting on data sets to show the current state of processing
- Inspecting a group of new data sets to make sure they have the expected structure
- Documenting a group of data sets that are ready for delivery
- Providing documentation on project data sets for new programmers and research scientists.

For each data set in the folder, %TK_inventory will capture information about the name, label, creation date, number of observations, and number of variables, and then print a report showing this information.

## Syntax

The %TK_inventory macro can be run with the following statement:

```
%TK_inventory(libref=libref_folder, output=inventory_list);
```

## Arguments

libref:              Required argument identifying the nickname assigned to the folder of SAS data sets by the LIBNAME statement.

output:             Optional argument specifying the name of an output data set containing the data that %TK_inventory creates to produce the data set inventory.

## Output Data Set

The following variables are returned in the output data set.

**Table 5-1: Variables in Output Data Set Used to Create Inventory of Data Sets**

| Variable | Type | Length | Label |
|---|---|---|---|
| setname | Char | 32 | SAS Data Set Name (*.sas7bdat) |
| memlabel | Char | 256 | Data Set Label |
| crdate | Num | 8 | Create Date (formatted DATETIME16.) |
| nobs | Num | 8 | Observations in Data Set |

| Variable | Type | Length | Label |
|----------|------|--------|-------|
| nvars | Num | 8 | Number of Variables |

## Example 5-1: Create an Inventory of Data Sets

The SAS code displayed in Program 5-1 illustrates how easy it is to create a complete enumeration of the SAS data sets in a folder.

*Section 1:* The statements in this section of the program create macro variables set to the names of folders for:

- The storage location of the SAS data for the project
- The *Data Detective's Toolkit* macro programs
- The output created by this program

The LIBNAME statement assigns nickname SAS_data to the project data and a nickname SAS_out to store output created by the SAS job. These nicknames are called libref in SAS terminology.

*Section 2:* This section creates a macro variable storing the date on which the inventory list was created. Using the WORDDATE12. format creates a value having the form "Month-name DD, YYYY." TITLE statements are created for your inventory report using macro variables. The date on which the inventory was run is recorded in TITLE3 by including macro variable &date_fmt. The location of the inventory is documented with TITLE4 by including macro variable &data_folder.

*Section 3:* The report showing the inventory of data sets is constructed in this last section. PROC TEMPLATE creates a template named custom based on the SAS style named ocean. The OPTIONS statements are used to create a report with a portrait orientation with 1.5 inch margins. The date and page numbers SAS will print are suppressed (options nodate nonumber). ODS is used to create a file with the RTF format using the custom template just created. The BODYTITLE OPTION in the ODS statement tells SAS to write the titles in the main part of the document rather than the header.

### Program 5-1: Create an Inventory of Data Sets

```
* Section 1) Define folders, library references for data, and include the
%TK_inventory.sas macro program;
%let TKFolder = /Data_Detective/Book/SAS_programs/TK_toolkit;
%let DataFolder = /Data_Detective/Book/SAS_Datasets;
%let WorkFolder = /Data_Detective/Book/SAS_Output;

libname SAS_out "&WorkFolder";
libname SAS_data "&DataFolder";

%include "&TKFolder./TK_inventory.sas";

* Section 2) Format date, add options to embellish titles and footnotes;
```

```
data _null_;
    today = trim(left(put(date(), worddate12.)));
    call symput ('date_fmt',today);
run;

title j=center height=12pt font=Arial Bold "Current Inventory of Health
Watch 2020 Data";
title3 j=left height=10pt font=Arial "Data Collected Through &date_fmt";
title4 j=left height=10pt font=Arial "Location: &DataFolder";


* Section 3) Create Inventory Table;

proc template;
    define style styles.custom;
        parent=styles.ocean;
        style bodyDate from bodyDate / font=('Times',10pt);
        style PagesDate from PagesDate / font=('Times',10pt);
        style PagesTitle from PagesTitle / font=('Times',10pt);
        style SystemTitle from SystemTitle / font=('Times',12pt);
        style Data from Data / font=('Times, Times, Times',10pt);
        style Header from HeadersAndFooters /
                font=('Times, Times, Times',10pt);
        style RowHeader from HeadersAndFooters /
                font=('Times, Times, Times',10pt);
end;
run;

options papersize=letter orientation=portrait leftmargin=1.5in
rightmargin=1.5in topmargin=1.5in bottommargin=1.5in;
options nodate nonumber;

ods rtf file="&WorkFolder./Inventory5_1.rtf" style=custom bodytitle;
%TK_inventory(libref=SAS_data, inv_output=Inventory);
ods rtf close;
```

The report created by the %TK_inventory macro is shown in Inventory 5-1. The output data set (Inventory) created when %TK_inventory was invoked is not shown here, but it can be used to customize the appearance of your report or establish a history of processing over time by saving your inventory report to folder with a name that includes the current processing date.

### Inventory 5-1: Current Inventory of SAS Data Sets in a Folder

#### Current Inventory of Health Watch 2020 Data

Data Collected Through Jul 21, 2020
Location: /Data_Detective/Book/SAS_Datasets

| SAS Data Set Name (*.sas7bdat) | Data Set Label | Create Date | Observations in Data Set | Number of Variables |
|---|---|---|---|---|
| DEMOGRAPHY | Final Demography Data for Study A | 05JUN20:16:32:46 | 501 | 8 |

| SAS Data Set Name (*.sas7bdat) | Data Set Label | Create Date | Observations in Data Set | Number of Variables |
|---|---|---|---|---|
| DEMOGRAPHY_A1 | Fictional Data from Study A, Collection 1 | 05JUN20:16:32:44 | 403 | 8 |
| DEMOGRAPHY_A2 | Fictional Data from Study A, Collection 2 | 05JUN20:16:32:45 | 98 | 8 |
| HEALTH | Health Data for Study A | 05JUN20:16:32:47 | 501 | 6 |
| HWS | Final Data for Healthy Worker Study | 17JUL20:14:13:38 | 501 | 20 |
| STUDYA | Final Data for Study A | 05JUN20:16:32:48 | 501 | 17 |
| STUDYA_PRELIM | Preliminary Data for Study A | 05JUN20:16:42:05 | 501 | 17 |
| STUDYA_RAW | Raw Data for Study A | 05JUN20:16:32:47 | 501 | 17 |
| TELEFORM_DATA | Test Teleform Data | 17JUL20:15:29:59 | 4 | 4 |
| WEB_DATA | Test Web Data | 17JUL20:15:29:59 | 7 | 4 |

## Inside the Toolkit: %TK_inventory

The %TK_inventory macro is a good example showing how easy it is to create a useful macro program using standard SAS statements enclosed with the %MACRO and %MEND statements. The source code for %TK_inventory is easy to understand and is discussed in this section.

The %MACRO statement shows two parameters used by %TK_inventory. The first parameter, &libref, is required and identifies the nickname for a folder that was defined in a LIBNAME statement earlier in the SAS job. The second parameter, &INV_OUTPUT, is optional and, if supplied, will be the name used to create a data set with the variables created for the Inventory Report.

```
%macro TK_inventory(libref=, inv_output=);
```

PROC DATASETS is used to create a data set with information about every SAS data set stored in the folder referenced by the &libref parameter. There is one observation for every variable in every data set in the output data set created by PROC DATASETS. Only four variables are needed to provide the information about a data set for the inventory. These variables are the data set name (MEMNAME), label (MEMLABEL), creation date (CRDATE), and number of observations (NOBS).

```
proc datasets lib=&libref noprint;
   contents data=_all_ out=work._ds_theInfo(keep=memname memlabel
         crdate nobs);
run;
```

PROC FREQ creates an output data set that shows the number of variables in each data set. The tables statement counts the number of variables in the data.

```
proc freq data=work._ds_theInfo noprint;
   tables memname*memlabel*crdate*nobs/list missing
      out=count(drop=percent rename=(count=NVARS memname=SETNAME));
run;
```

The next DATA step prepares the data set for printing before sorting by setname.

```
data _ds_thefiles;
   set count;
   setname=upcase(setname);
   label NVARS='Number of Variables';
   label SetName='SAS Data Set Name (*.sas7bdat)';
run;

proc sort data=_ds_thefiles;
   by setname;
run;
```

The inventory report is printed with PROC REPORT.

```
proc report data=_ds_thefiles nocenter nowindows headline wrap missing
   style(header)=[color=black ];
   column  setname memlabel crdate nobs nvars;
   define memlabel/display  width=50;
   define crdate/display center width=15;
   define nobs/display center width=10 missing;
   define nvars/display center width=10 missing;
   format nobs comma15.0;
run;
```

The macro %IF statement that follows determines whether you provided a name for a data set to store the variables created for the inventory report. If the macro variable &INV_OUTPUT is not missing, then an output data set will be created.

```
%if "&inv_output" ^= "" %then
   %do;
      data &inv_output(label="Inventory data set for &DataFolder");
      retain setname memlabel crdate nobs nvars;
      set _ds_thefiles;
      run;
   %end;
```

The last task for the %TK_inventory macro is to remove the temporary data sets created.

```
proc datasets noprint;
   delete _ds_thefiles _ds_theInfo;
run;

%mend;
```

# Using the %TK_xwalk Macro

A crosswalk is a table that maps the variables in one data set into the equivalent variables in one or more other data sets. Thus, a crosswalk shows the "union" (all variables in all sets) as well as the "intersection" (variables in common) of multiple data sets.

The %TK_xwalk macro considers variables in multiple data sets to be the same if they have identical names and provides additional information about differences in variable label, format, and data type. It can be used to uncover the relationship between variables in multiple files.

Ideally, the data sets you include in your crosstab report will be cleaned data sets ready to analyze. For the data scientist, the report created by %TK_xwalk provides a useful reference displaying all variables in a group of data sets and identifying the data set(s) in which the variables are located. Variables in data sets that have conflicting attributes of label, data type, or format can be easily discovered in the crosstab table produced by %TK_xtab and provides an early warning to the data scientist or programmer needing to work with these data sets.

## Syntax

```
%TK_xwalk(SetList = SAS_data1.set1 SAS_data2.set2 SAS_data3.set3 · · · );
```

## Arguments

SetList: List of any number of data sets. Separate each data set by a space. For example, libref1.set1 libref2.set2 libref3.set3 libref4.set4 etc.

## Example 5-2: Creating a Crosswalk

This example examines three sets of data and determines which variables exist in all sets, in one set, or a group of sets by creating a crosswalk. These data sets have some inconsistencies and issues to illustrate how the crosswalk can be used for quality control or investigative purposes when needing to combine multiple of data sets. This example creates a report with the RTF format, but programmers might find creating a report with an Excel format is better for large numbers of data sets.

To run the %TK_xwalk macro, you only need to provide a list of the data sets to be included in the crosswalk, separating each name by blanks. Note that each data set is specified by both the libref and data set name. This allows the data sets to be in one or more folders, with the folders identified by the libref defined with the LIBNAME statement. The code shown in Program 5-2 specifies three data sets to use to create the crosswalk.

*Section 1:* Similar to Program 5-1, this section defines macro variables for each folder that will be accessed in the SAS job, uses the LIBNAME statement to define a libref nickname for two folders:

- F1: the folder containing two of the data sets
- F2: the folder containing one of the data sets
- SAS_out: the folder where the crosstab output report will be saved

Each libref nickname is used along with the name of the associated SAS data set in columns of the crosstab report.

*Section 2:* Titles created in this section are useful documentation for your crosstab report. TITLE4 creates a heading for folders where data sets are stored. TITLE5 creates a title that identifies the folder associated with the libref SAS_data. If your data sets are stored in more than one folder, then add an additional TITLE statement for each libref to display the folder names.

*Section 3:* The crosswalk report is created in *Section 3* with RTF format using landscape orientation. The SAS "statistical" style is used for formatting with no modifications. The BODYTITLE OPTION is used to write the title of the report in the body of the report rather than the header of the RTF document. Crosswalks can get quite wide if many data sets are used in the crosstab, so Excel would be an excellent choice for these reports.

### Program 5-2: Create a Crosswalk for Multiple Data Sets

```
* Section 1) Define folders, library references for data, and include
Inventory program;
%let TKFolder = /Data_Detective/Book/SAS_programs/TK_toolkit;
%let DataFolder = /Data_Detective/Book/SAS_Datasets;
%let RawData = /Data_Detective/Book/SAS_RawData;
%let WorkFolder = /Data_Detective/Book/SAS_Output;
libname SAS_out "&WorkFolder";
libname F1 "&DataFolder";
libname F2 "&RawData";

%include "&TKFolder./TK_xwalk.sas";

* Section 2) Create titles;
title j=center height=12pt font=Arial Bold
    "Crosswalk Comparing Variables in Multiple Data Sets";
title3 j=left underlin=1 "Location of data sets:";
title5 "F1 = &DataFolder";
title6 "F2 = &RawData";

* Section 3) Create Crosswalk and save report;
options orientation=landscape;
ods RTF file="&WorkFolder./CrossWalk5_2.rtf" style=statistical bodytitle;

%TK_xwalk( SetList = F1.studya F2.demog F1.health );
run;
```

The output created by %TK_xwalk appears in the Crosswalk 5-2. The first column on the left contains the names of variables in all three data sets. Here is what you can tell from the structure of this crosswalk about the relationship between the sets:

- The first row labeled "Total" indicates there is a total of 31 variables in the 3 sets, with 8 in the demography data set, 6 in the health data set, and 17 in the third data set. Some of these variables have the same names.

- The first column shows the names of variables from one or more of the data sets. Some of these variables appear in multiple sets, so there is actually only 15 unique variable names in the three sets.

- An entry of "1" in any of the last three columns indicates that the variable is present in that data set. Note that the only variable present in all three data sets is CASEID.

- The column labeled "Total/Frequency" reports the number of data sets with variables of the same name having the matching attributes
  - Label
  - Type-Length (data type)
  - Format values

Crosswalk 5-2: Crosswalk Comparing Variables in Multiple Data Sets

**Crosswalk Comparing Variables in Multiple Data Sets**

<u>**Location of data sets:**</u>

**F1 = /Data_Detective/Book/SAS_Datasets**
**F2 = /Data_Detective/Book/SAS_RawData**

| VARIABLE CROSSWALK | | | | Total | Data Set | | |
| --- | --- | --- | --- | --- | --- | --- | --- |
| | | | | | F1.health | F1.studya | F2.demog |
| | | | | Frequency | Frequency | Frequency | Frequency |
| Total | | | | 32 | 6 | 17 | 9 |
| Variable Name | Variable Label | Type-Length | Variable Format | | | | |
| AGE | Age at interview date | NUM-8 | | 2 | . | 1 | 1 |
| BIRTHDATE | Date of birth | NUM-8 | MMDDYY | 2 | . | 1 | 1 |
| CASEID | Unique identifier for participant | NUM-8 | | 3 | 1 | 1 | 1 |
| CHG_WEIGHT | What are you trying to do about your weight? | CHAR-8 | $SHOWALL | 1 | . | . | 1 |
| | | NUM-8 | | 1 | 1 | . | . |
| | | | CHG_WT | 1 | . | 1 | . |
| CITY | Fictional city where participant lives | CHAR-20 | | 2 | . | 1 | 1 |
| DURATION | | NUM-8 | | 1 | . | 1 | . |
| EXER_DAYS | In the Past 30 days, how many days did you exercise at least 30 minutes? | NUM-8 | | 2 | 1 | 1 | . |
| HEALTH | | NUM-8 | | 1 | 1 | . | . |

| VARIABLE CROSSWALK | | | | Total | Data Set | | |
|---|---|---|---|---|---|---|---|
| | | | | | F1.health | F1.studya | F2.demog |
| | | | | Frequency | Frequency | Frequency | Frequency |
| | How is your health? | | HEALTH | 1 | . | 1 | . |
| INT_DATE | Interview date | NUM-8 | MMDDYY | 2 | . | 1 | 1 |
| LANGUAGE | Language | NUM-8 | | 1 | . | 1 | . |
| MODE | Mode of data collection | CHAR-4 | $MODE | 2 | . | 1 | 1 |
| NUM_DOC_VISITS | Number of doctor visits past year | NUM-8 | | 1 | . | 1 | . |
| RACE | Race/Ethnicity | NUM-8 | RACE | 2 | . | 1 | 1 |
| SEX | Gender | NUM-8 | SEX | 1 | . | . | 1 |
| | Sex of participant | NUM-8 | SEX | 1 | . | 1 | . |
| SMOKE | Do you currently smoke? | NUM-8 | | 2 | 1 | 1 | . |
| STATUS | Interview Status | NUM-8 | | 1 | . | 1 | . |
| WEIGHT | How would you describe your weight? | NUM-8 | | 1 | 1 | . | . |
| | | | WEIGHT | 1 | . | 1 | . |

Variables having the same name and matching attributes in the crosswalk include:

- The CASEID variable appearing in all three data sets. Since the label documents that it is a unique identifier for each participant in the study and has matching attributes, it is likely to be a variable that you could use to merge the data sets.

- Some variables such as AGE, BIRTHDATE, CITY, EXER_DAYS, INT_DATE, MODE, RACE, and SMOKE appear in two of the data sets and have the same data type and assigned format.

- Other variables are in only one of the three data sets such DURATION, LANGUAGE, and STATUS appear in only F1.studya.

One helpful feature of the crosswalk table is that variables having the same name in multiple data sets but different attributes can be easily discovered. These differences can indicate that the variables have different meanings in the data sets.

The cell where a difference occurs in any of the attributes will be split for the different values of the attributes. Looking at the rows in the table for a variable where an attribute cell was split will help you identify possible differences in the meaning of a variable located in different data sets.

For example, split cells in Crosswalk 5-2 indicate these variables will need to be investigated before the data sets are combined:

- The CHG_WEIGHT variable appears in all three data sets but has unique attributes in each set
    - Numeric data type in the F1.HEALTH and F1.STUDYA data sets, but character in the F2.DEMOG data set
    - Different assigned formats for the F1.STUDYA and F2.DEMOG data sets, no assigned format in the F1.HEALTH data set.
- The HEALTH variable has an assigned format in the F1.STUDYA data set but no assigned format in F1.HEALTH
- The SEX variable has different labels in the F1.STUDYA and F2.DEMOG data sets
- The WEIGHT variable has a FORMAT assigned in the F1.STUDYA data set, but not in the F1.HEALTH data set.

The %TK_xwalk tool is an extremely useful tool to uncover variables that are common to multiple data sets by creating a crosswalk showing the relationship of variables across all data sets. This example has illustrated how %TK_xwalk can uncover inconsistencies in the data sets that will need to be investigated before these sets can be easily used for analysis. The %TK_harmony data tool can also be used to uncover these consistencies and is designed to be used specifically for finding inconsistencies in two data sets that need to be merged or concatenated. %TK_Harmony will be covered in Chapter 6. For variables with the same name and data type having differences in storage length identified by %TK_harmony or %TK_xwalk, the %TK_max_length macro covered in Chapter 2 can be used to assign the maximum storage length when you combine data sets.

## Inside the Toolkit: %TK_xwalk

The %TK_xwalk macro program loops through each data set in the SetList parameter included in your crosswalk. It extracts information from PROC CONTENTS to create the crosswalk. PROC TABULATE is used to create the actual crosswalk table. This macro has less than 60 lines of code and is a good example showing how to use macro statements to loop through a list of items and consolidate information about each item. The source code for %TK_xwalk is explained in the remainder of this section.

The macro program is defined by the %MACRO and %MEND statements. The second statement in the macro uses the %LOCAL statement to define two macro variables, &i and &next_name, as local variables so that they will only be available to the macro program.

```
%macro %TK_xwalk(SetList=);
    %local i next_name;
```

The %DO iterative statement creates the macro variable &i and uses the %SYSFUNC macro function to execute the SAS function COUNTW determining the maximum number of items in &SetList. A space is used as a delimiter to count the number of items.

```
%do i=1 %to %sysfunc(countw(&setlist,%str( )));
```

The %LET statement creates macro variable &next_name by selecting one of the items in &SetList. The value of macro variable &i determines which data set is selected.

```
%let next_name = %scan(&setlist,&i, %str( ));
```

An output data set named _xw_info_ extracted from PROC CONTENTS contains all the information needed for the crosstab about the data set being inspected. PROC CONTENTS creates an observation about every variable in the data set.

```
proc contents data=&next_name noprint out=_xw_info_(keep=nobs
    libname memname name label type length format);
```

Next, a DATA step is used to either create (first time through %DO loop) or append the output data from PROC CONTENTS to create the data set (_xw_thevars_ ) needed for constructing the crosstab report.

```
data _xw_thevars_;
    %if &i = 1 %then
        %do;
            set _xw_info_ (in=in_info);
        %end;
    %else
        %do;
            set _xw_thevars_ _xw_info_ (in=in_info);
        %end;
```

For each observation added to the crosstab data set, a variable is created by combining length and type information (VARTYPE), saving the name of the data set being processed (WHICH_SET), and saving the position of the data set in &SetList (NUMBER). Labels are created for each of these new variables.

```
length vartype $ 10;
length which_set $ 32;

if in_info then
    do;
        if type=1 then
            vartype=compress("NUM-"||length);
        else if type=2 then
            vartype=compress("CHAR-"||length);
        number=&i;
        which_set = "&next_name";
    end;
```

```
label which_set='Data Set';
      label memname='Data Set Name (*.sas7bdat)';
      label vartype='Type-Length';
      name=upcase(name);
  run;

%end;
```

The last statement in the DATA step sets the value stored in variable NAME to uppercase before using PROC TABULATE to create the crosswalk table.

```
proc tabulate data=_xw_thevars_(keep= nobs memname which_set name label
      type length format vartype) missing;
  class _all_;
  tables all name*label*vartype*format , (all which_set)/rts=15
      box='VARIABLE CROSSWALK';
  keylabel n='Frequency';
  keylabel all='Total';
run;
```

The last step is to cleanup the SAS workspace by deleting the data sets created by %TK_xwalk. Note that each name of these data sets begins and ends with an underscore ( _ ) to differentiate the name from data sets you might create.

```
proc datasets noprint;
  delete _xw_thevars_ _xw_info_;
run;

%mend;
```

# Summary

Good documentation is essential for understanding and using project data. Chapters 3, 4, and 5 presented useful data management tools that automatically create documentation for understanding your project data. Generating these documents is easy and automated, making it practical to incorporate creating them into your normal routine.

Always having up-to-date codebooks, crosswalks, and inventories of data sets gives you a great way to "know your data." These documents do a great job of highlighting mistakes and unexpected results. You will find mistakes and correct them before they become a problem.

Not only are these data tools useful for data sets your team is creating, but they are also useful to use on data that you receive, especially if the data that you receive is not well-documented.

# Chapter 6: Detecting and Correcting Data Errors

## Introduction

Data sets contain available facts and information providing evidence whether a belief or hypothesis is true. During collection, inconsistencies and anomalies can occur in the raw data that must be resolved to make your data ready to be used to answer questions. Unexpected missing values, incorrect flow through skip patterns, incomplete data, and combining multiple data sets with different attributes all require careful investigation and alleviation during data preparation. Data cleansing is an iterative and interactive process that programmers ideally perform both during and after collection. While this can be a time-consuming and costly task, the *Data Detective's Toolkit* provides SAS macro programs to automate much of the detective work normally performed during data cleansing, thereby reducing the time spent editing and validating data.

The %TK_codebook data tool covered in Chapter 3 automatically detected the following issues in your data set:

- Discovered variables that have out of range values

- Reported variables that have 100% missing values

- Identified variables that have missing labels or no assigned format

This chapter teaches you how to use the Toolkit to aid and automate the following tasks during data cleansing:

- Harmonize multiple data sets to ensure that information is not compromised when they are combined by using %TK_harmony

- Determine observations that have duplicate values of identification variables using %TK_find_dups

Adding the capabilities of these two macro data tools to the potential problem reports from %TK_codebook provides easy to use and comprehensive ways to clean your data.

# Harmonizing Data Sets: Using the %TK_harmony Macro

Often your data will come from many different sources and files. One example is a survey that is collected with different modes of collection such as web versus teleform. Although the data sets contain the same questions, data sets from the different modes might not always be created with the same structure. The task to combine data from all sources into one set by concatenating or merging requires the sets have identical data attributes for variables with the same name. If you have variables with the same name but different attributes such as data type, data length, label or assigned format, then combining these data sets can compromise the integrity of these variables.

The %TK_harmony macro compares the structure of two data sets and reports on differences found in data type and label of the variables having the same name, and identifies variables that are unique to each set. This information is needed to harmonize the data so that the data sets can be combined into one set without errors. Any differences in data type, data length, label, or assigned format should be reconciled before the data sets are combined.

## Syntax

The macro %TK_harmony can be run with the following statement:

```
%TK_harmony(set1 = data_set_name1,
            set1_id = set_abbreviation1,
            set2 = data_set_name2,
            set2_id = set_abbreviation2,
            out = output_set);
```

## Required Arguments

set1        Name of first data set

set1_id     Short nickname (maximum of 20 characters) for first data set name used in
            output report

set2        Name of second data set

set2_id     Short nickname (maximum of 20 characters) of second data set name used in output report


## Optional Arguments

out         Name of output data set


## Output Data Set

The contents of the optional output data set is listed in Table 6-1. Attributes of all variables from both data sets are included.

**Table 6-1: Variables Included in Optional Output Data Set from %TK_Harmony**

| Variable | Type | Length | Label |
|---|---|---|---|
| harmony | Char | 10 | Harmony measure comparing type, length, and label of variable (Values: DIFF = different, SAME = All Match, SOLO = variable in only one file) |
| label1 | Char | 256 | *set1_id* variable label |
| label2 | Char | 256 | *set2_id* variable label |
| label_match | Char | 3 | Both have same variable label? (Values: Yes, No) |
| Location | Char | 20 | File location of variable (Values: Both, *set1_id*, *set2_id*) |
| Name | Char | 32 | Variable name |
| type_length1 | Char | 9 | *set1_id* variable data type (Num, Char) and length |
| type_length2 | Char | 9 | *set2_id* variable data type (Num, Char) and length |
| type_match | Char | 3 | Both have same data type? (Values: Yes, No) |


# Example 6-1: Harmonizing Two Data Sets

The demographic data in this example were collected by both web and teleform. Before concatenating these files, Program 6-1 shows how we can use the %TK_harmony macro to identify differences that might compromise data integrity when combining the data sets.

## Program 6-1: SAS Program to Find Differences in Attributes of Variables in Two Data Sets

```
options nocenter noreplace nofmterr symbolgen mprint;

* Section #1) Define folders, library references for data, and include
TK_harmony.sas macro program;
%let TKFolder = /Data_Detective/Book/SAS_programs/TK_toolkit;
%let DataFolder = /Data_Detective/Book/SAS_Datasets;
%let WorkFolder = /Data_Detective/Book/SAS_Output;
libname SAS_out "&WorkFolder";
libname SAS_data "&DataFolder";

%include "&TKFolder./TK_harmony.sas";

* Section #2) Create Harmony Table;
title 'Harmony of data sets for Study A, Collection 1 and 2';
options papersize=letter orientation=portrait leftmargin=1.5in
rightmargin=1.5in topmargin=1.5in bottommargin=1.5in;
ods rtf file="&WorkFolder./Harmony6_1.rtf" style = festival bodytitle;

%TK_harmony(set1= SAS_data.demography_a1,
      set1_id=Web,
      set2= SAS_data.demography_a2,
      set2_id=Paper,
      out=harmony_results);
run;

ods rtf close;
```

*Section 1:* The SAS code in this part of the program creates macro variables containing the names of folders accessed in the SAS job, defines the libref assigned to the folders, and includes the %TK_harmony macro as part of the job stream.

*Section 2:* This part of the %TK_harmony macro runs a comparison of two data sets (SAS_data.demography_a1 and SAS_data.demography_a2), assigns nicknames of Web and Paper to these data sets, and obtains an output data set named HARMONY_RESULTS. Tables created by %TK_harmony are written to an RTF file named Harmony6_1.rtf using the Festival style sheet.

The first table (Summary 6-1) printed by %TK_harmony shows a summary of the harmony measures for the variables that have the same name in both data sets, and identifies variables that appear in only one data set.

## Summary 6-1: Summary Showing Harmony of Data Sets for Study A, Collection 1 and 2

| Harmony of Variables: Web=SAS_data.demography_a1 and Paper=SAS_data.demography_a2 | | | | Total | |
|---|---|---|---|---|---|
| | | | | N | Percent |
| Harmony measure | Variable location | Both have same data type? | Both have same variable label? | | |
| DIFF | Both | No | Yes | 1 | 11.11 |
| | | Yes | No | 2 | 22.22 |

| Harmony of Variables: Web=SAS_data.demography_a1 and Paper=SAS_data.demography_a2 | | | | Total | |
|---|---|---|---|---|---|
| | | | | N | Percent |
| SAME | Both | Yes | Yes | 4 | 44.44 |
| SOLO | Paper | N/A | N/A | 1 | 11.11 |
| | Web | N/A | N/A | 1 | 11.11 |
| Total | | | | 9 | 100.00 |

The two data sets have nine variables with unique names. Seven of these variables (harmony measure equals DIFF or SAME) have identical names in both data sets while two of the variables (harmony measure equals SOLO) are found in only one of the data sets.

For the variables that have the harmony measure of DIFF (different data type or label), SAME (matching data type and label), or SOLO (in one set only):

- Four have the same data type and label (Harmony=SAME)
- One has the same label, but different data type (Harmony=DIFF)
- Two have the same data type, but different label (Harmony=DIFF)
- Two variables occur in only one of the data sets (Harmony=SOLO)

The variables with Harmony=SAME do not need further investigation for combining the two data sets. The next table (Details 6-1) printed by %TK_harmony shows details of the variables with harmony measure equal DIFF or SOLO. There are three attributes in this table that indicate differences:

- LOCATION indicating which data file(s) have a variable with this name
- DATA TYPE combining both NUMeric or CHARacter specification with storage length for each file where the variable was found
- LABEL comparing the SAS LABEL assigned to the variable from each data file

Attributes of each variable that need investigating are printed in bold and highlighted. From this report we can tell the following differences need to be corrected when the two data sets are concatenated:

- AGE and SEX have different labels in the two data sets
- MODE has different data types (CHAR 3 vs CHAR 4) in the two data sets
- The Web data set has a variable CTIY, which is likely to be a misspelling of the variable CITY.

## Details 6-1: Differences in Attributes of Data Sets for Study A, Collection 1 and 2

| Web=SAS_data.demography_a1<br>Paper=SAS_data.demography_a2<br><br>Inharmonic Variables | | | Data Type | | | Label | | |
|---|---|---|---|---|---|---|---|---|
| Harmony Measure | Variable name | Variable Location | Same? | Web | Paper | Same? | Web | Paper |
| DIFF | AGE | Both | Yes | NUM 8 | NUM 8 | No | Age at interview date | Age of participant |
| SOLO | CITY | Paper | N/A | | CHAR 20 | N/A | | Fictional city where participant lives |
| SOLO | CTIY | Web | N/A | CHAR 20 | | N/A | Fictional city where participant lives | |
| DIFF | MODE | Both | No | CHAR 3 | CHAR 4 | Yes | Mode of data collection | Mode of data collection |
| DIFF | SEX | Both | Yes | NUM 8 | NUM 8 | No | Gender | Sex of participant |

The differences in attributes identified in this table can be handled with SAS statements shown in Program 6-2.

## Program 6-2: SAS Program to Combine Data Sets for Study A, Collection 1 and 2

```
data demography;
   length mode $ 4;
   set SAS_data.demography_a1 (rename=(ctiy = city) )
       SAS_data.demography_a2;
   label age = "Age of participant at interview date";
   label sex = "Sex of participant";
run;
```

The problems that could occur when concatenating the web and teleform data sets are avoided by using the following simple SAS code to concatenate the data sets:

- The LENGTH statement appearing before the SET statement will avoid any possible truncation of data for the MODE variable by taking the larger storage length of the variable in the two sets to use in the LENGTH statement. You could also use the %TK_max_length macro covered in Chapter 2 in section "Using the *Data Detective's Toolkit* Macro Programs" to discover the maximum storage length needed for the LENGTH statement.

- The misspelled variable CTIY was renamed with the correct spelling CITY.

- Differences for labels for variables AGE and SEX were amended.

# Inside the Toolkit: How %TK_harmony Works

The %TK_harmony program uses standard SAS code sandwiched between the %MACRO and %MEND statements creating a reusable macro program to harmonize two data sets. This makes it easy to understand, and would also be easy for you to modify if you wanted the macro to have additional capabilities. The macro code is explained in the remainder of this section.

The %TK_harmony macro uses four required keyword parameters to identify the names of data sets (set1=, set2=), nicknames or abbreviations for the data sets (set1_id=, set2_id=) for annotating harmony reports, and an optional keyword parameter to get an output data set.

```
%macro tk_harmony(set1=, set1_id=, set2=, set2_id=, out=);
```

The next statement will suppress procedure-specific titles (PROC FREQ, PROC CONTENTS, etc.) for being written to the ODS output destinations.

```
ods noproctitle;

proc format;
   value vartype 1='NUM' 2='CHAR' .=' ';
run;
```

PROC CONTENTS is used next to obtain information about the variable attributes in each data set.

```
* Step 1) Create data set with measures of harmony;
proc contents data=&set1 noprint out=_info1(keep=label length name
     type varnum);
run;

proc contents data=&set2 noprint out=_info2(keep=label length name
     type varnum);
run;
```

The variable NAME in each data set output from PROC CONTENTS is changed to be uppercase before sorting each data set by NAME.

```
data _info1;
   set _info1;
   name=upcase(name);
run;

data _info2;
   set _info2;
   name=upcase(name);
run;

proc sort data=_info1;
   by name;
run;

proc sort data=_info2;
   by name;
run;
```

This DATA step first defines lengths of character variables that will be created for evaluating the harmony measures used to compare the two files.

```
data _join_;
    length harmony $ 10;
    length type_match $ 3;
    length label_match $ 3;
    length location $20;
```

The MERGE statement renames select variables in each data set to unique names before merging by variable NAME.

```
    merge _info1(in=in1 rename=(label=label1 length=length1 type=type1
        varnum=varnum1))
        _info2(in=in2 rename=(label=label2 length=length2 type=type2
                varnum=varnum2));
    by name;
```

The LENGTH and TYPE of each variable reported by PROC CONTENTS is used to create a new composite variable that simplifies creating the harmony reports.

```
    length type_length1 $9 type_length2 $9;

    if not missing(type1) and not missing(length1) then
        type_length1= compress(put(type1,vartype.))||' ' ||
                    compress(length1);
    else type_length1=' ';

    if not missing(type2) and not missing(length2) then
        type_length2= compress(put(type2,vartype.))||' '||
                    compress(length2);
    else type_length2=' ';
```

A variable named LOCATION is created to determine in which data set each variable resides.

```
    if in1 and in2 then
        location="Both";
    else if in1 and not in2 then
        location="&set1_id ";
    else if in2 and not in1 then
        location="&set2_id ";
```

If found in both data sets, the label and data type of a variable from each set are compared to assess if there are any differences in the attributes of a variable across the two data sets.

```
    if in1 and in2 then
        do;
            if compress(upcase(label1))=compress(upcase(label2)) then
                label_match='Yes';
            else label_match='No';

            if type1=type2 and length1=length2 then
                type_match='Yes';
            else type_match='No';
        end;
    else
        do;
```

```
            label_match = 'N/A';
            type_match='N/A';
        end;
```

The overall HARMONY measure is created next for each variable with the following IF-THEN-ELSE statement.

```
    if in1 and in2 and type_match='Yes' and label_match='Yes' then
        harmony='SAME';
    else if in1 and in2 and (type_match='No' or label_match='No') then
        harmony='DIFF';
    else if in1 and not in2 then
        harmony='SOLO';
    else if in2 and not in1 then
        harmony='SOLO';
```

The labels are created for each variable, using the short names for the data set in the last four label statements.

```
        label location="Variable location";
        label harmony="Harmony measure comparing type, length, and label of
variable (DIFF = different, SAME = All Match, SOLO = variable in only one
file";
        label label_match="Both have same variable label?";
        label type_match="Both have same data type?";
        label type_length1="Data type for &set1_id";
        label type_length2="Data type for &set2_id";
        label label1 = "Label for &set1_id";
        label label2 = "Label for &set2_id";
    run;
```

The next part of the macro uses PROC TABULATE to write a summary report of the harmony measures created in the previous DATA step.

```
    *Step 2) Write Report;
    proc tabulate data=_join_ missing;
        class harmony location type_match label_match;

        table harmony*location*type_match*label_match all,
            all*(n*f=8. reppctn) /rts=10
            box="Harmony of Variables: &set1_id=&set1 and &set2_id=&set2";
        keylabel RepPctN = 'Percent';
        keylabel all = 'Total';
        label harmony = 'Harmony measure';
    run;
```

PROC REPORT is used to write a report focusing on only those variables with differences in attributes across the two data sets being compared.

```
    proc report data=_join_ headline wrap split="~";
        where harmony in ('SOLO', 'DIFF');
        column (" &set1_id=&set1 ~ &set2_id=&set2 ~ ~ Inharmonic Variables"
            harmony name location)
            ('Data Type' type_match type_length1 type_length2)
            ('Label' label_match label1 label2);
        define harmony / display "Harmony Measure" center;
        define name / display "Variable name" center;
```

```
define location / display "Variable Location" center;
define type_match / display "Same?" center;
define type_length1 / display "&set1_id" center
       style(column)={tagattr="format:@"};
define type_length2 / display "&set2_id" center
       style(column)={tagattr="format:@"};
define label_match / display 'Same?' center;
define label1 / display "&set1_id" center;
define label2 /display "&set2_id" center;
```

The following compute blocks highlight cells to accentuate attributes that differ or need to be investigated for each variable. Yellow highlighting is chosen for "SOLO" harmony values while light red highlighting is used for variable attributes that do not match in the two data sets.

```
compute harmony;

   if harmony = "SOLO" then
      do;
          call define(_col_, "style", "style=[fontweight=bold
              backgroundcolor = very light yellow]");
      end;
endcomp;


compute name;

   if harmony = "SOLO" then
      do;
          call define(_col_, "style", "style=[fontweight=bold
              backgroundcolor = very light yellow]");
      end;
endcomp;


compute type_match;

   if type_match = "No" then
      do;
          call define(_col_, "style", "style=[fontweight=bold
              backgroundcolor = light red]");
      end;
endcomp;


compute type_length1;

   if type_match = "No" then
      do;
          call define(_col_, "style", "style=[fontweight=bold
              backgroundcolor = light red]");
      end;
endcomp;


compute type_length2;

   if type_match = "No" then
      do;
          call define(_col_, "style", "style=[fontweight=bold
              backgroundcolor = light red]");
      end;
endcomp;
```

```
    compute label_match;

        if label_match = "No" then
            do;
                call define(_col_, "style", "style=[fontweight=bold
                    backgroundcolor = light red]");
            end;
    endcomp;

    compute label1;

        if label_match = "No" then
            do;
                call define(_col_, "style", "style=[fontweight=bold
                    backgroundcolor = light red]");
            end;
    endcomp;

    compute label2;

        if label_match = "No" then
            do;
                call define(_col_, "style", "style=[fontweight=bold
                    backgroundcolor = light red]");
            end;
    endcomp;
run;
```

If requested, an output data set is created with the next part of the SAS program.

```
    * Step 3) Create output data set if requested;
    %if "&out" ^="" %then
        %do;

            data &out (label="Harmony measure for &set1 (&set1_id) vs &set2
(&set2_id)");
                set _join_;
                label location="Variable location";
                label harmony="Harmony measure comparing type, length, and
label of variable (DIFF = different, SAME = All Match, SOLO = variable in
only one file)";
                label name = "Variable Name";
                label label_match="Both have same variable label?";
                label type_match="Both have same data type?";
                label type_length1="&set1_id variable data type (Num, Char)
and length";
                label type_length2="Data type for &set2_id variable data type
(Num, Char) and length";
                label label1 = "&set1_id variable label";
                label label2 = "&set2_id variable label";
                keep location harmony name label_match type_match type_length1
                    type_length2 label1 label2;
            run;

        %end;
```

PROC DATASETS is used to delete the temporary data sets created by this macro.

```
proc datasets noprint;
delete _info1 _info2 _join_;
run;
```

ODS PROCTITLE statement is used to allow SAS procedure titles to be written to any ODS destinations that are used after the macro ends.

```
   ods proctitle;
%mend;
```

# Finding Duplicates: Using the %TK_find_dups Macro

An important step in data preparation is to ensure variables that uniquely identify an observation occur only on one observation. The %TK_find_dups macro examines a data set and reports on any observations that have the same value of one variable or a list of key variables separated by asterisks. An optional output data set is available containing the values of the key variables that occur on more than one observation. Any formats assigned to the variables are ignored in the examination.

## Syntax

The %TK_find_dups macro can be run with the following statement:

%TK_find_dups(dataset=*data_set_name*, one_rec_per=*variable_list*, dup_output=*output_set*);

### Required Arguments

dataset:                      Name of SAS data set to be examined.

one_rec_per:              Variable or list of variables separated by asterisks.

### Optional Arguments

dup_output:      Output data set for the variables specified in the parameter ONE_REC_PER that have that values occurring on more than one observation in the data set.

# Example 6-2: Identifying Duplicates Based on Multiple Variables

This example illustrates how to identify duplicates based on any subset of variables in your data set using the %TK_find_dups macro. Program 6-3 shows how easy it is to do this. The goal of the final data set STUDY is to have one observation for every unique value for variables CASEID*WAVE.

**Program 6-3: Example Program to Identify Duplicates Based on a Subset of Variables**

```
* Section #1) Define folders, library references for data, and include data
tool to find duplicate observations;
%let TKFolder = /Data_Detective/Book/SAS_programs/TK_toolkit;
%let DataFolder = /Data_Detective/Book/SAS_Datasets;
%let WorkFolder = /Data_Detective/Book/SAS_Output;
libname SAS_out "&WorkFolder";
libname SAS_data "&DataFolder";

%include "&TKFolder./TK_find_dups.sas";

* Section #2) Create a data set with some duplicate observations;
data STUDY;
    input CASEID WAVE LOCATION STATUS $;
    label CASEID = 'Unique identifier for participant';
    label WAVE = 'Wave of data collection';
    label LOCATION = 'Location of interview';
    label STATUS = "STATUS (C=Complete/P=Partial)";
    datalines;
100  1    4    C
100  2    4    C
100  3    4    C
200  1    6    P
200  1    6    P
200  1    6    C
200  2    3    C
300  1    5    C
300  2    5    C
300  3    5    C
400  1    6    C
400  2    6    C
400  2    6    C
;

* Section #3) Find duplicate observations in data set (if they exist);
title  'Find Records with Duplicate Values of Identification Variables in
Data Set';
ods rtf file= "&WorkFolder./Duplicates6_2.rtf" style=htmlblue;

%TK_find_dups(dataset=work.STUDY, one_rec_per=CASEID*WAVE,
dup_output=STUDY_DUPS);
run;

* Section #4) Print all duplicates;
data extract_dups;
    merge STUDY STUDY_DUPS (in=in_dups);
    by caseid wave;

    if in_dups;
run;

proc print data=extract_dups label;
    by caseid copies;
    var caseid wave location status;
run;
```

```
ods rtf close;
ods listing;
run;
```

*Section 1:* This section of the program uses SAS code to define macro variables to hold the names of the folders used in the example. Next, LIBNAME statements create a libref assigned to the data folder and the output folder. An %INCLUDE statement reads the source code of the macro and includes it as part of the SAS job.

*Section 2:* This part of the program creates a SAS data set that has a few duplicate observations based on the variables CASEID and WAVE. Typically, your data would have many more variables than the four variables used to create this set. The variable STATUS is included here because it contains useful information that will help determine which observation is the most reliable for research.

*Section 3:* The following statements run macro %TK_find_dups to examine data set STUDY for any occurrences of multiple observations with identical vaiues of CASEID*WAVE. An output data set named STUDY_DUPS is requested.

*Section 4:* The last few statements in the program use the output data set from %TK_find_dups to extract only the duplicated observations from the original data set.

The first table created by %TK_find_dups appears in Summary 6-2. There are 10 unique values of CASEID* WAVE in the 13 observations in data set STUDY. This table shows there are eight observations that have unique values of CASEID*WAVE, two observations that have the same value of CASEID*WAVE, and three observations that have the same value of CASEID*WAVE.

**Summary 6-2: Findings from the %TK_find_dups Examination of the Data Set STUDY**

Data set being examined:  work.STUDY (N=13)
Identification variables:  CASEID*WAVE
There should be only one record for every unique value of CASEID*WAVE

**COPIES = Number of records with identical values of CASEID*WAVE**

| COPIES | Frequency | Percent | Cumulative Frequency | Cumulative Percent |
|--------|-----------|---------|---------------------|--------------------|
| 1 | 8 | 80.00 | 8 | 80.00 |
| 2 | 1 | 10.00 | 9 | 90.00 |
| 3 | 1 | 10.00 | 10 | 100.00 |

The next table shown in Details 6-2 shows the values of CASEID*WAVE that occur multiple times in the data set. CASEID = 200 has three observations with values of WAVE=1 while CASEID=400 has two observations with values of WAVE=2. This table is used to create the optional output data set that can be requested by using the "dup_output=" parameter when the %TK_find_dups macro is invoked.

## Details 6-2: Details Showing Actual Values of CASEID*WAVE for Duplicate Observations

Values of CASEID*WAVE occurring on more than one record in data set work.STUDY
COPIES = Number of records with identical values of CASEID*WAVE

| CASEID | WAVE | COPIES | Frequency |
|---|---|---|---|
| 200 | 1 | 3 | 1 |
| 400 | 2 | 2 | 1 |

The actual records that were extracted by the SAS program statements in *Section 4* of
%TK_find_dups are listed in the two tables shown in Duplicates 6-2.

## Duplicates 6-1: Duplicate Records Found in Data Set

Unique identifier for participant=200 Number of records with identical values of CASEID*WAVE=3

| Obs | Unique identifier for participant | Wave of data collection | Location of interview | STATUS (C=Complete/P=Partial) |
|---|---|---|---|---|
| 1 | 200 | 1 | 6 | P |
| 2 | 200 | 1 | 6 | P |
| 3 | 200 | 1 | 6 | C |

Unique identifier for participant=400 Number of records with identical values of
CASEID*WAVE=2

| Obs | Unique identifier for participant | Wave of data collection | Location of interview | STATUS (C=Complete/P=Partial) |
|---|---|---|---|---|
| 4 | 400 | 2 | 6 | C |
| 5 | 400 | 2 | 6 | C |

The next step would be to examine the full record for each participant at every wave to
determine which of the records is the most complete data to keep. For participant with
CASEID=200, only one of the records has STATUS=C indicating the data collection was
completed. The partial surveys might be multiple attempts to complete the survey with the
partial attempts being stored in the data. There are two complete records for participant = 400
indicating that a completed survey was entered twice.

# Inside the Toolkit: How %TK_find_dups Works

The source code for the %TK_find_dups macro is shown below. This macro includes required
keyword parameters to specify the name of the input data set (dataset=) and variables that

uniquely identify an observation (one_rec_per=) in the data set. An optional parameter can be used to request an output data set with values of those variables for duplicated observations.

```
%macro tk_find_dups(dataset=, one_rec_per=, dup_output=);
   ods noproctitle;
```

The FREQ PROCEDURE is used to find the number of duplicates by computing the number of observations having unique values for the variables that are designed to identify a single observation. Using the FORMAT _ALL_ statement requests that SAS ignore the formats assigned to variables in the data set specified by macro variable &DATASET for the duration of the PROC FREQ step. This uses the actual values stored in the variable rather than the formatted values when creating the table.

```
proc freq data=&dataset noprint;
   tables &one_rec_per/list missing
         out=_dup_check_ (rename=(count=COPIES));
   format _all_;
run;
```

The next statement uses the macro function %SYSFUNC to execute a SAS function. The OPEN function is used here to open a SAS data set and return a unique numeric data set identifier needed to use other functions that access the data set. OPEN returns a value of 0 if the data set cannot be opened.

```
%let dsid=%sysfunc(open(&dataset));
```

If the data set was opened, then %SYSFUNC creates a macro variable named &NUMOBS with the number of observations in the data set, and then closes the data set.

```
%if &dsid %then
   %do;
      %let numobs=%sysfunc(attrn(&dsid,nlobsf));
      %let rc=%sysfunc(close(&dsid));
   %end;
```

The ODS text statements use macro variables to annotate the report that is being created.

```
ods escapechar='^';
ods text = "Data set being examined: &dataset (N=&numobs)";
ods text - "Identification variables: &one_rec_per";
ods text = "There should be only one record for every unique value of
&one_rec_per";
ods text = "^1n";
```

PROC FREQ is used to print the first table in the report showing the number of copies in the data set having unique values of the identification variables.

```
proc freq data=_dup_check_;
   tables copies/list missing;
   label copies="COPIES = Number of records with identical values of
&one_rec_per";
      format _all_;
   run;
```

The data is subset to only those values of the identification variables that have duplicates.

```
data _the_dups_ ;
   set _dup_check_;

   if copies>1;
run;
```

The OPEN function is used once more to determine the number of observations in the data set (_the_dups_) just created. If there are 0 observations, then a message is printed to the SAS log reporting that there is only one record for every unique value of the identification variables. The %RETURN statement causes a normal termination of the %TK_find_dups macro.

```
%let dsid=%sysfunc(open(_the_dups_));

%if &dsid %then
   %do;
      %let numobs=%sysfunc(attrn(&dsid,nlobsf));
      %let rc=%sysfunc(close(&dsid));
   %end;

%if &numobs=0 %then
   %do;
      %put NOTE: No duplicates, Only one record per &one_rec_per in
&dataset data set.;

      %return;
   %end;
```

If duplicates were found, a warning message is printed in the SAS log, then the macro prints a second table in the report.

```
%put WARN: Duplicates found by TK_find_dups, Multiple records have same
value of &one_rec_per in &dataset data set.;
   ods text = "Values of &one_rec_per occurring on more than one record in
data set &dataset";
   ods text = "COPIES = Number of records with identical values of
&one_rec_per";
   ods text = "^1n";

   proc freq data=_the_dups_;
      tables &one_rec_per*copies /list missing nocum nofreq nopercent
nocol;
      format _all_;
   run;

   title3 ' ';

%if "&dup_output" ^= "" %then
   %do;
```

If requested, an output data set is created using the data set containing the values of the identification variables that are duplicated.

```
      data &dup_output (label="Values of &one_rec_per for duplicate
observations in &dataset" drop=percent);
```

```
          set _the_dups_;
          label copies = "Number of records with identical values of
&one_rec_per";
       run;

   %end;
```

PROC DATASETS is used to clean up the work space by deleting the data sets %TK_find_dups created.

```
   proc datasets noprint;
      delete _DUP_CHECK_ _THE_DUPS_;
   run;

   ods proctitle;
%mend;
```

## Summary

The value of your data is enhanced when you detect and correct anomalies before the data is distributed to users. This chapter has illustrated simple ways to detect anomalies in your data before they become problems. The %TK_find_dups macro detects observations that have duplicate identification variables in your data set while the %TK_harmony macro identifies inconsistency and incompatibility in the structure of variables from two different data sets.

Although %TK_harmony, %TK_find_dups, and %TK_codebook are very simple data tools to use, they are very powerful tools to use for monitoring and improving quality of your data.

# Chapter 7: Inspect and Edit Flow through Skip Patterns

## Introduction

Skip patterns are commonly used in surveys to ensure that only relevant questions are asked of each participant. Your role as a programmer is to validate the data flowing through a skip pattern. The first step is to uncover any contradictory responses and incorrect flow of the data through each skip pattern. Once you identify any problems that occur, your next step is to replace each inconsistent value with a substitute value that maintains the integrity of the participant's data. This can make your job of checking and repairing skip patterns very arduous. The %TK_skip_edit macro greatly reduces this burden.

This chapter teaches you how to validate variables that are part of a skip pattern and recommend ways to edit incorrect flow through a skip pattern. You will learn how to use the %TK_skip_edit macro data tool to automate the most demanding tasks involved in checking skip paths:

- Creating and inspecting a crosstab table to audit the flow of data through the skip pattern and identify spurious, inconsistent, or contradictory data values.

- Automate editing the value of any variables that have spurious or contradictory data values because of incorrect flow through a skip pattern.

# Understanding Skip Patterns

Skip patterns built into surveys reduce the time for a participant to fill out the survey, lowering costs for data collection and increasing the willingness of the participant to complete the survey. Logic built into the design of the survey identifies which questions are appropriate for the participant based on prior responses in the survey. Using this information, a computerized survey will automatically skip questions that do not need to be asked for each participant. For web or computer-based surveys, the participant never sees the omitted questions, allowing very complex skip patterns to be built into the survey.

The source code programmers write for web and computerized surveys can be very involved and early versions might have mistakes causing inconsistencies in the flow of data through the skip pattern. Inconsistencies can also happen if a participant decides to change their answers in a survey. For example, some computerized surveys allow users to back up to change their response to a question. Here is what can happen with the collected data when this involves a skip pattern:

- The first time through a survey a question is displayed only if it is determined to be applicable to the participant from responses to prior questions.

- If the question is displayed and the participant answers, the computerized survey records the answer.

- If the participant decides to back up in the survey to change a response to a prior question, inconsistencies can arise.

    ○ The participant can change their response to a question controlling the skip pattern.

    ○ If the question is no longer applicable, it will not be displayed as the participant continues with the survey.

    ○ The participant's original answer remains stored in the computer memory causing inconsistencies in the flow of data through the skip pattern.

For teleform or paper surveys, the responsibility of understanding the flow of questions and answering only what is applicable to each participant lies solely on the participant. Even instructions to follow simple skip patterns can confuse participants trying to fill out teleform or paper surveys, leading to confusing and inconsistent responses in their data.

Your job as a programmer is to find the mistakes and inconsistencies early before they can become problems. If possible, you should find mistakes in the instruments either during testing of the data collection instruments or during the pilot survey. Inconsistencies that arise from participants backing up in the survey or confusion by a participant filling out a paper or teleform survey should be cleaned up before the data is used. This can make your job of validating skip patterns in the data quite challenging and time consuming.

The survey might not be final at this stage, with questions removed, added, or renamed. Skip patterns can change. All of these improvements to the survey cause continual updates in your SAS program written to examine the skip patterns. The traditional methods used to inspect how well the collected data follows the intended skip pattern can result in very complicated SAS code. Even the simplest changes in the survey can result in very complicated and time-consuming changes in your original SAS program. The %TK_skip_edit macro will significantly reduce the amount of SAS code that you write to examine and fix skip patterns.

## Identifying Skip Patterns in a Survey

The questions shown in Survey 7-1a to Survey 7-1c involve skip paths common in many surveys. Arrows have been drawn on the survey to have a visual display of the skip pattern used to determine whether each question is relevant to the participant answering the question.

The demographic questions in Part 1 are asked for all participants.

Part 2 of the survey captures tobacco use for participants. Those who have never smoked a cigarette, not even just one or two puffs are skipped to Part 3 of the survey. Questions TOB2 through TOB4 are asked of all participants who reported cigarette smoking in TOB1. TOB5 is asked of only current smokers as determined from TOB1 and TOB2.

Pregnancy history is recorded in Part 3 of the survey. The arrows show that every question in this section is involved in a skip pattern. The pregnancy questions should only be answered by female participants. Question PG1 determines whether the female participant has ever had a pregnancy. Those reporting no pregnancies skip to the end of the survey. Question PG3 was added to version 2 of the survey increasing the complexity of determining how well the data flows through the skip pattern. Question PG5 is asked only to those women who are sure they are currently pregnant.

Data from this survey will be used extensively in the examples in this section. This data has been simulated and contains mistakes to illustrate the methods of checking skip patterns and illustrating the capabilities of the %TK_skip_edit macro tool.

Survey 7-1a: Part 1: Demographics

**PART 1: DEMOGRAPHICS**

**DEM1.   How old are you?**

|__|__| Age [RANGE 18-99]

**DEM2. Which of the following best describes you? (*Please select one answer*.)**

1 ☐ Female
2 ☐ Male

**DEM3. What is your race? Please select one or more.**

1 ☐ White
2 ☐ Black or African American
3 ☐ Hispanic
4 ☐ Asian
5 ☐ Other
6 ☐ Refused

**DEM4. What is the highest grade or year of school you have completed?**

1 ☐ Less than high school
2 ☐ High school graduate or GED
3 ☐ Some college/vocational school (no degree)
4 ☐ 2-year college/vocational/Associate's degree
5 ☐ 4-year college degree or higher (e.g., BA, BS, MA, MS, Ph.D)

Survey 7-1b: Part 2: Tobacco Use

## PART 2: TOBACCO USE

**TOB1.** Have you ever smoked a cigarette, even one or two puffs?

1 ☐ Yes
2 ☐ No → GO TO PART 3 ———————— TOB1 = 2 → PG1 (Part 3)

[ASK IF TOB1 = 1]
**TOB2.** On how many of the past 30 days did you smoke a cigarette?

|__|__| Days [RANGE 0-30]

[ASK IF TOB1 = 1]
**TOB3. Have you smoked at least 100 cigarettes in your entire life?**

1 ☐ Yes
2 ☐ No

[ASK IF TOB1 = 1]
**TOB4. During the past 12 months, have you stopped smoking cigarettes for one day or longer because you were trying to quit smoking cigarettes?**

1 ☐ Yes
2 ☐ No

[ASK IF CURRENT CIGARETTE SMOKER (TOB1=1 and TOB2>0) ; ELSE GO TO PART 3]
**TOB5. In the next 3 months, do you think you will...**(*Please select one answer*):

1 ☐ Smoke the same amount of cigarettes that you do now    TOB1=2
2 ☐ Increase the amount of cigarettes that you smoke    OR
     TOB2=0 →
3 ☐ Decrease the amount of cigarettes that you smoke    PG1 (Part 3)
4 ☐ Quit smoking cigarettes altogether

TOB1 = 2 → PG1 (Part 3)

Part 3

## Survey 7-1c: Part 3: Pregnancy History

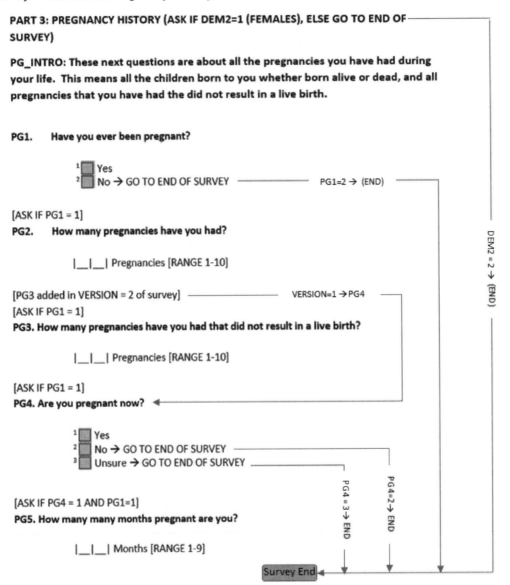

**PART 3: PREGNANCY HISTORY (ASK IF DEM2=1 (FEMALES), ELSE GO TO END OF SURVEY)**

**PG_INTRO: These next questions are about all the pregnancies you have had during your life. This means all the children born to you whether born alive or dead, and all pregnancies that you have had the did not result in a live birth.**

**PG1.    Have you ever been pregnant?**

¹ ☐ Yes
² ☐ No → GO TO END OF SURVEY ———————— PG1=2 → (END)

[ASK IF PG1 = 1]
**PG2.    How many pregnancies have you had?**

|__|__| Pregnancies [RANGE 1-10]

[PG3 added in VERSION = 2 of survey] ———————— VERSION=1 → PG4
[ASK IF PG1 = 1]
**PG3. How many pregnancies have you had that did not result in a live birth?**

|__|__| Pregnancies [RANGE 1-10]

[ASK IF PG1 = 1]
**PG4. Are you pregnant now?** ◄

¹ ☐ Yes
² ☐ No → GO TO END OF SURVEY
³ ☐ Unsure → GO TO END OF SURVEY

[ASK IF PG4 = 1 AND PG1=1]
**PG5. How many many months pregnant are you?**

|__|__| Months [RANGE 1-9]

PG4 = 3 → END
PG4=2 → END
DEM2 = 2 → (END)

Survey End ◄

# Traditional Method of Auditing Skip Patterns

The traditional way to examine a skip pattern is to create and inspect a crosstab of each variable being skipped with the variables causing the skipping. You will be looking for deviations from the expected flow of data values. If deviations are identified, a DATA step is commonly used to edit data values to mitigate problems. The crosstab to examine question TOB5 asking "In the next 3 months, do you think you will…" has four possible responses and is asked for current smokers.

Current smokers are determined from questions TOB1 "Have you ever smoked a cigarette?" and TOB2 "On how many of the past 30 days did you smoke a cigarette?" The SAS code to create this crosstab is quite simple and is shown below:

**Program 7-1: Examine Skip Pattern**

```
proc format;
     value TOB2f 0='0' 1-30 = "1-30";
run;

proc freq data=SAS_data.skippatterndata;
     tables TOB5*TOB2*TOB1/list missing;
     format TOB5 TOB1;
     format TOB2 TOB2f.;
run;
```

The Crosstab 7-1 shows the output from this code.

**Crosstab 7-1: Visual Inspection Evaluating TOB5 Skip Pattern**

| Comments from Visual Inspection | TOB5 | TOB2 | TOB1 | Frequency | Percent |
|---|---|---|---|---|---|
| OK: Never Smoked (TOB1=2) | . | . | 2 | 352 | 50.21 |
| MISSING: Expected reply for TOB5 | . | 1-30 | 1 | 39 | 5.56 |
| OK: Never Smoked (TOB1=2) BAD: TOB2 should not have a value | . | 1-30 | 2 | 7 | 1.00 |
| BAD: TOB5 should not have a value (Not current smoker fromTOB2=0) | 1 | 0 | 1 | 3 | 0.43 |
| OK | 1 | 1-30 | 1 | 175 | 24.96 |
| BAD: TOB5 should not have a value (Not current smoker fromTOB2=0) | 2 | 0 | 1 | 2 | 0.29 |
| OK | 2 | 1-30 | 1 | 75 | 10.70 |
| OK | 3 | 1-30 | 1 | 23 | 3.28 |
| BAD: TOB5 should not have a value (Not current smoker fromTOB2=0) | 4 | 0 | 1 | 1 | 0.14 |
| OK | 4 | 1-30 | 1 | 24 | 3.42 |

From the questionnaire TOB5 should be skipped if TOB1= 2 or TOB2=0. The first column of the crosstab shows how this information is used to evaluate the flow of data through the skip pattern. Comments in the first column of the table indicate where inconsistencies show up in the flow through the data from TOB1 to TOB5. From this table you can see 39 of the participants did not answer TOB5 when they were expected to answer, and another six participants had inconsistent and confusing (BAD) flow on the path going from question TOB1 to TOB5. Programming and printed instructions for the data collection instrument should be checked.

If this is actual data to be used, then editing will be necessary to make the data usable. The next step would be to write a SAS program to change the values of TOB5 and TOB2 to values that do not compromise the flow of the data through the TOB1 to TOB5 skip pattern. A common rule used to edit inconsistent responses is to replace the inconsistent value with a missing data value or a special value outside the valid range for each variable. Using a special value like -99 can be documented to represent a missing value, but this value will need to be recoded before the variable can be used in analysis.

Using a SAS missing data value can avoid a lot of recoding when the data is later analyzed with SAS. In addition to using a period (.) to indicate that a numeric value is missing SAS provides special numeric missing values. These special missing values are represented by a single period followed by a single letter or an underscore (for example, .A, .S, .Z, ._). SAS code to assign a special missing value is very simple and is shown in Program 7-2 The special SAS missing value ".E" is assigned to indicate a status of "Expected Reply" and a ".L" assigned to mean Legitimate Skip.

SAS has a special MISSING Statement that can be used to assign characters occurring in numeric variables in your input data set to represent special missing values when your data in being read into your program. Because Program 7-2 uses an assignment statement to recode the data to special SAS missing values (TOB2=.L) after it is read into the DATA step, no MISSING statement is needed. Here are guidelines to creating special missing values:

- To use special missing numeric values in a SAS expression or assignment statement, begin the value with a period followed by an uppercase letter, lowercase letter, or an underscore.

- Only an uppercase letter is displayed when SAS prints a special missing value.

- When you are reading in a data that has characters in a numeric field and you want those characters interpreted as special missing values, include the MISSING statement in your program.

## Program 7-2: Edit Data Values Using Special Missing Values

```
data fix_data;
    set SAS_data.skippatterndata;

    if TOB1=2 then
        do;
            TOB2=.L;
            TOB5=.L;
        end;

    if TOB2=0 then
        TOB5=.L;

    if TOB1 = 1 and 1<=TOB2<=30 and missing (TOB5) then
        TOB5 = .E;
run;

proc freq data=fix_data;
    tables TOB5*TOB2*TOB1/list missing nocum;
    format TOB5 TOB1;
```

```
    format TOB2 TOB2f.;
run;
```

Crosstab 7-2 displays the table showing the data after editing.

**Crosstab 7-2: Data after Editing to Correct Inconsistent Flow Through Skip Path for Variable TOB5**

| Comments from Visual Inspection | TOB5 | TOB2 | TOB1 | Frequency | Percent |
|---|---|---|---|---|---|
| Expected Reply to TOB 5 | E | 1-30 | 1 | 39 | 5.56 |
| Legitimate Skip (Never smoked) | L | L | 2 | 359 | 51.21 |
| Legitimate Skip (Not Current Smoker) | L | 0 | 1 | 6 | 0.86 |
| OK | 1 | 1-30 | 1 | 175 | 24.96 |
| OK | 2 | 1-30 | 1 | 75 | 10.70 |
| OK | 3 | 1-30 | 1 | 23 | 3.28 |
| OK | 4 | 1-30 | 1 | 24 | 3.42 |

Assigning special values to indicate why something is missing can provide useful information to understand the reason the data value was missing. This helps the analyst determine the best way to handle the missing data.

Common reasons why a value is missing are listed below:

- Response to question can be inferred from prior questions (Legitimate Skip)
- Question is not applicable to participant filling out survey (Legitimate Skip)
- Participant did not answer question even though it was presented (Expected Response)
- Question was added to survey after participant's interview was completed (Question Not Available)

Although the DATA step statements and running PROC FREQ are not complicated programming, the task to do the visual inspection to identify inconsistent flow through skip patterns can be labor intensive, especially because you might have hundreds of skip patterns to examine. The task of translating the editing logic to SAS is very exacting, then a new crosstab needs to be created and examined. To really determine whether your SAS program statements edited the data as desired, you would need to merge the original and edited data to create a crosstab showing original data and edited data. This would make a more complex table to examine.

# Example 7-1: Using the %TK_skip_edit Macro

The %TK_skip_edit macro can simplify the process of validating skip patterns and reduce the amount of time that you spend inspecting each variable for inconsistent flow through a skip pattern. It requires you to set up formats that identify the values of a variable that control the flow through a skip pattern. This information is then used to determine whether the variable that you are checking should be skipped based on the variables designated as controlling the skip. Here is what you need to provide %TK_skip_edit to evaluate a skip pattern for each variable:

- The name of the variable that you are investigating to determine how it flows through the skip pattern (CHECK_VAR)
- All variables that can trigger skipping the variable that you want to evaluate (SKIP_VARS)
- Formats that identify values that trigger a skip in the questionnaire by using the word SKIP embedded in the value label (SKIP_FMTS).

Using this information, the %TK_skip_edit macro automatically performs the following tasks for evaluating the flow through the skip pattern:

- An annotated crosstab classifying how combinations of values of the SKIP_VARS are associated with the presence or absence of a value for the CHECK_VAR
  - OK: Value is present when question should be asked, missing when question should be skipped
  - BAD: ANSWERED, SHOULD SKIP: Value is present and should be missing
  - BAD: EXPECTED REPLY, NO ANSWER: Value is missing and should have been answered
- Editing of the data when needed to have the following default values
  - Legitimate Skip (.L ) – Variable was or should have been legitimately skipped
  - Expected Reply (.E) – Variable was missing but a response was expected from the participant
- Tally of edits showing the number of observations needing editing for each variable examined by %TK_skip_edit
  - Count of observations where CHECK_VAR did not need editing because of incorrect flow through the skip pattern
  - Count of observations where CHECK_VAR was edited to .L (Legitimate Skip) because a nonmissing value was found when CHECK_VAR should have been missing
  - Count of observations where CHECK_VAR was edited to .E (Expected Reply) because a missing value was found when the participant should have answered the question

%TK_skip_edit macro inspects a crosstabulation of each variable involved in a skip pattern, first looking for deviations from the expected flow of data values, and then editing the data using the logic programmed into the macro described earlier in this chapter. You also have flexibility in changing the default values of ".L" and ".E" used in editing the data to a value that might work better for your particular project.

## Syntax

The %TK_skip_edit macro can be run with the following statement:

```
%TK_skip_edit( check_var=,
        skip_vars=,
        skip_fmts=,
        subgroup=,
        strata_var=,
        strata_fmt=,
        Legit_Skip=.L,
        Expect_Reply=.E,
        print_xtab=YES,
        tally_edits=YES);
```

## Required Arguments

check_var:      Variable being checked for missing value pattern and possible editing

skip_vars:      Variables that control if question is expected to be answered by the participant, separated by an asterisk (*). Read "How Skip Path Logic is Implemented by %TK_skip_edit" to understand how SKIP_VARS is interpreted for assessing if CHECK_VAR was skipped.

skip_fmts:      Name of each variable in the SKIP_VARS list followed by a name of the format identifying values that control skipping the question. Read "Skip Formats" for instructions on creating the formats.

## Optional Arguments

subgroup:       SAS Boolean logic syntax to specify a subgroup of observations to apply the skip logic

strata_var:     Variable to stratify the crosstab table that shows editing results and edit status for variable being checked by %TK_skip_edit

strata_fmt:     Name of stratification variable followed by the name of a format defining the categories of the strata

Legit_Skip:     Value to be used for editing inconsistent values of numeric variables to Legitimate Skip (default = .L) Inconsistent character values are edited to a blank " "

Expect_Reply:   Value to be used for editing inconsistent numeric values to Expected Reply (default =.E) )

print_xtab:     Print crosstab showing RECODED_VAR*ORIGINAL_VAR*SKIP_VARS to check how recoding was done (default = YES)

tally_edits:    Tally the number of times a variable needed editing to correct flow (default = YES). These statistics will be saved in a data set with a name of your choice. Use the statement %LET TALLY_RESULTS = *tally_statistics* where tally_statistics is a name of your choice for this data set.

## Tally Results Data Set

The %TK_skip_edit macro creates a data set summarizing the edits performed on your raw data set. To create this data set you need to provide a name for the data set by using the following statement in your SAS program:

```
%let tally_results = My_Results;
```

The %LET TALLY_RESULTS= statement saves the results from every following invocation of %TK_skip_edit macro to a data set named My_Results. To change the name of the data set capturing these results, just issue another %LET TALLY_RESULTS= statement in your program with a different data set name. The saved results include a summary of any edits performed on the variable (CHECK_VAR) being checked. You can choose any valid name for a SAS data set to use in place of My_Results.

Section 5 of Program 7-3 shows you how to use this data set to print summary reports Crosstab 7-3 and 7-4 for the survey in described in "Identifying Skip Patterns in a Survey."

**Table 7-1: Variables in Output Data Set Created Using %LET TALLY_RESULTS = My_Results**

| Variable Name | Type | Label |
|---|---|---|
| CHECK_VAR | Char | Variable Checked |
| EXPECT_REPLY | Char | Value used to recode Expected Reply |
| LEGIT_SKIP | Char | Value used to recode Legitimate Skip |
| SKIP_FMTS | Char | Formats Assigned to Skip Variables |
| SKIP_VARS | Char | Variables Directing Skip Pattern Flow |
| STRATA_VAR | Char | Strata Variable |
| SUBGROUP | Char | Subset of Data Examined |
| SVY_MODE | Num | Value of variable passed to &strata_var, label of variable passed to &strata_var is used for label of SVY_MODE |

| Variable Name | Type | Label |
| --- | --- | --- |
| COUNT | Num | Frequency Count |
| SKIP_STATUS | Num | Skip Pattern Edit Status<br>This Value indicates edit performed on variable being checked and has the following values:<br><br>0 = OK: Missing when should be skipped, edit value to Legitimate Skip value (assigned in parameter LEGIT_SKIP)<br><br>1 = OK: Answered when Expected Reply, then value is unchanged<br><br>2 = BAD: Answered when should have been skipped, edit value to Legitimate Skip value (assigned in parameter LEGIT_SKIP)<br><br>3 = BAD: Missing when reply expected, then edit value to Expected Reply value (assigned in parameter EXPECT_REPLY) |

[1] Source is from user-supplied value to PARAMETER of %TK_skip_edit invocation, while DERIVED is based on a calculation from %TK_skip_edit invocation.

## Skip Formats

%TK_skip_edit uses the format assigned to a skip variable to determine what values should trigger skipping the variable being checked. The formats that you create need to be structured in a specific way for %TK_skip_edit to correctly identify the values that trigger skipping. Below are examples of the formats that will work:

```
proc format;
    value SKIP0f 0='0=SKIP';
    value SKIP1f 1='1=SKIP';
    value SKIP2f 2='2=SKIP';
    value SKIP3f 3='3=SKIP';
    value SKIP1_2f 1='1=SKIP' 2='2=SKIP';
    value SKIP2_3f 2='2=SKIP' 3='3=SKIP';
    value SKIP3_4f 3='3=SKIP' 4='4=SKIP';
    value TOB2SKIP 0='0=SKIP' 1-30 = "1-30=ask";
run;
```

The structure needed for your formats to work for %TK_skip_edit is simple. The word SKIP needs to occur in the value label following an equal (=) sign. You can use either upper or lowercase. There should be only one equal sign in the value label, and nothing following the word SKIP within the text description. These formats are also used to annotate the crosstab table created to trace the flow of data through the skip pattern. Including the value that triggers skipping the variable assigned to the format helps make the crosstab table easier to understand. Any formats permanently assigned to variables in your data set will not be replaced with these formats. In some cases, a missing value found for questions that the participant did not answer should cause questions that follow to be skipped. For %TK_skip_edit to handle this situation, you should include missing values in a format to indicate that the missing value triggers skipping other questions (variables) later in the survey. For example:

```
value SKIP3_missf 3='3=SKIP'.='.=SKIP' .L='.L=SKIP';
```

would tell %TK_skip_edit that values of 3 and SAS missing (. or .L) will cause a variable to be skipped.

## How Skip Path Logic Is Implemented by %TK_skip_edit

The parameters SKIP_VARS and SKIP_FMTS are used in tandem to determine whether a question should be skipped based on responses to prior questions. For example, question PG2 "How many pregnancies have you had" shown in SURVEY 7-1c is skipped for participants who are male (DEM2=2) OR women who have never been pregnant (PG1=2). The %TK_skip_edit statement to evaluate how all participants flow through the skip pattern and perform needed edits would be:

```
%TK_skip_edit(check_var = PG2,
              skip_vars = DEM2*PG1,
              skip_fmts = DEM2 skip2f. PG1 skip2f.);
```

Each of the skip variables listed in parameter SKIP_VARS is evaluated using the assigned format in SKIP_FMTS. By doing this, %TK_skip_edit determines whether the value stored for a participant's skip variable triggers skipping CHECK_VAR, the variable being checked. This is equivalent to mathematically combining the binary SKIP status of the skip variables with Boolean logic operator OR. To compute if the current value triggers a skip, the format assigned to each SKIP variable is used to identify if the value of the SKIP variable indicates the participant should not answer the corresponding question. Below is the SAS code that you would have to write to accomplish what this one call to %TK_skip_edit accomplishes:

```
/*OK (Male or Never Pregnant): Legitimate Skip*/
if ((DEM2=2 or PG1=2) and PG2=.) then
    do;
        PG2 = .L;
        status="OK ";
    end;

/*BAD (Male or Never Pregnant): Answered PG2, should skip*/
else if ((DEM2=2 or PG1=2) and not missing(PG2)) then
    do;
        PG2=.L;
        status="BAD";
    end;

/*OK (Female and Ever Pregnant, or missing): KEEP original answer*/
else if (DEM2 in (1,.) and PG1 in (1,.)) and not missing (PG2) then
    do;
        status="OK ";
    end;

/*BAD(Female and Ever Pregnant, or missing: Expected Reply, No answer*/
else if (DEM2 in (1,.) and PG1 in (1,.)) and missing (PG2) then
    do;
```

```
        PG2=.E;
        status="BAD";
    end;
```

Another useful feature of the %TK_skip_edit macro is to limit the skip pattern examination and recoding to a subset of the observations in your data set by using the SUBGROUP parameter. The mathematical expression provided in the SUBGROUP parameter restricts the evaluation process to only those observations that share the conditions described by the mathematical expression. This gives the SUBGROUP mathematical expression the action of the Boolean logic operator AND. For example, question PG3 shown in SURVEY 7-1c was added in version 2 of the questionnaire and is asked only of females who have ever been pregnant. A separate %TK_skip_edit statement would be used for the participants who filled out Version=1 of the survey and those who filled out Version=2 or later. For the Version=1 participants, it would be useful to use a Legitimate Skip code of .N (rather than .L) to indicate that this question was Not Available when they filled out the survey. The %TK_skip_edit statement would be:

```
%TK_skip_edit(check_var = PG3,
            skip_vars = VERSION,
            skip_fmts = VERSION skip1f. ,
            subgroup = Version=1,
            legit_skip=.N);
```

The Boolean logic used by %TK_skip_edit would be:

```
if (VERSION=1) and missing (PG3) then PG3=.N;
```

The next %TK_skip_edit statement will examine the observations in the data set for participants who filled out version 2 and later of the survey.

```
%TK_skip_edit(check_var = PG3,
            skip_vars = VERSION*DEM2*PG1,
            skip_fmts = VERSION skip1f. DEM2 skip2f. PG1 skip2f.,
            subgroup = Version>1);
```

This skip pattern is identical to the skip pattern for PG2 for participants who were administered surveys later than version 1. This Boolean logic for this %TK_skip_edit would be:

```
/*OK: Legitimate Skip*/
if (VERSION>1 and (DEM2=2 or PG1=2) and PG3=.) then
    do;
        PG3 = .L;
        status="OK ";
    end;

/*BAD: Answered PG3, should skip*/
else if (VERSION>1 and DEM2=2 or PG1=2) and not missing(PG3) then
    do;
        PG3=.L;
        status="BAD";
    end;

/*OK: KEEP original answer*/
    else if (VERSION>1 and DEM2 in (1,.) and PG1 in (1,.)) and not missing
(PG3) then
        do;
```

```
        status="OK ";
   end;

/*BAD: Expected Reply, No answer*/
else if (VERSION>1 and DEM2 in (1,.) and PG1 in (1,.)) and missing
(PG3) then
   do;
      PG3=.E;
      status="BAD";
   end;
```

You can see how much easier it is to write the %TK_skip_edit statement rather than all the SAS code in a DATA step to do the same cleaning of the skip pattern.

Occasionally a survey will have extremely complex skip patterns involving dozens of variables controlling if a question is asked vs skipped. These complex skip patterns might involve elaborate Boolean logic beyond what %TK_skip_edit is designed to evaluate. For these types of skip patterns, use a DATA step to break down the elaborate Boolean logic by creating one or more variables that simplifies but still represents the original Boolean logic expression. Use these new variables with %TK_skip_edit to evaluate and recode the skip pattern. Including these variables in the final data set would be useful to analysts using your data.

# A Blueprint to Using %TK_skip_edit

Evaluating skip patterns in your survey is one of the more complicated tasks in preparing your data set. This makes using %TK_skip_edit appear more complex than the other data tools. This is because it can require more steps to set up the initial SAS job to evaluate and edit all the skip patterns in your data set. Before you write your SAS job, do the following steps to understand the skip patterns that you will be evaluating:

- Identify all skip patterns in a copy of the data collection instrument for your survey.

- It can be helpful to draw arrows on the survey to have a visual representation of the skip pattern.

- Review how the skip patterns were delineated in Survey 7-1a to 7-1c.

You are now ready to create your SAS job. The following steps provide a blueprint to what your SAS job should look like:

1.  DEFINE SAS ENVIRONMENT: Set up the environment for your SAS job:

    ○ OPTIONS statement as needed

    ○ LIBNAME statement to assign a libref to the folder where the data was located

    ○ %INCLUDE statement to include the TK_skip_edit.sas source code as part of your SAS job

2.  MAKE SKIP FORMATS: Create formats that include the word "SKIP" as part of the label assigned to each value causing one or more questions to be skipped as the participant

fills out the survey. See section on "SKIP FORMATS" for examples showing skip formats that work for the %TK_skip_edit macro.

3.  CREATE TEMPORARY DATA SET: Create a temporary version of your data set that the %TK_skip_edit macro can edit.

4.  DEFINE TEMPORARY DATA SET NAME: Store the name of the temporary data set in a macro variable called &OUTPUT_SET with the following SAS command:

    ○   %LET OUTPUT_SET= *temp_data_set;*

5.  SAVE CROSSTABS OF RESULTS: If you want to have the crosstabs showing the results of %TK_skip_edit for variables being checked saved in a file, then use the ODS statement to route output to the file. Here is an example:

    ○   ODS RTF FILE='/myfolder/edit_crosstab.rtf';

6.  COLLECT SUMMARY STATISTICS: If you want to see a summary of the edits once you have completed evaluating your skip paths with %TK_skip_edit, create a macro variable named &TALLY_RESULTS with the name of a data set used to accumulate summary statistics for each variable checked:

    ○   %LET TALLY_RESULTS = *Your_Tally_file;*

7.  CHECK VARIABLES: Use the %TK_skip_edit macro to check each variable in every skip pattern in your data set. Refer to the discussion on syntax earlier in the chapter for details about the parameters in the following statement:

    ○   %TK_skip_edit( check_var=*Variable being checked,*
        skip_vars=*Variables controlling skips,*
        skip_fmts=*Skip formats assigned to skip variables,*
        subgroup=*Expression defining subset to apply skip evaluation,*
        strata_var=*Stratification variable used only in Crosstabs and Summary statistics,*
        strata_fmt =*Format assigned to strata format,*
        Legit_Skip=.L, Expect_Reply=.E,
        print_xtab=YES, tally_edits=YES);

8.  CLOSE CROSSTAB OF RESULTS: If you defined an ODS file in step 5 to save the crosstabs, then close the ODS destination to the file when all the CHECKS in step 7 are done. Here is an example statement to close the ODS destination:

    ○   ODS RTF CLOSE;

9.  PRINT TALLY RESULTS: Print the summary statistics saved in the file &TALLY_RESULTS defined in step 6. The following PROC TABULATE can be used to print the summary and is explained in Example 7-2.

    ○   proc tabulate data=part3_tally missing;
        class check_var skip_status STRATA_var subgroup;
        var count;
        tables (check_var*subgroup=" "),
            (skip_status all)*COUNT=" "*(SUM=' '*F=6.0)/row=float;

```
        format skip_status TK_status.;
        format svy_mode mode.;
        run;
```

# Example 7-2: Automated Method of Checking Skip Patterns

This example uses simulated data from the questions displayed in Survey 7-1a to Survey 7-1c to automate evaluating and editing of skip patterns. The annotated arrows running along the right side of the questions provide a visual display of the skip patterns that you need to check. The SAS program shown in Program 7-3 translates these skip patterns into the proper syntax for %TK_skip_edit to examine and edit the data. This data has many problems that need to be mitigated.

*Section 1:* This section defines the folders used in the example, library references for the SAS data, and includes the %TK_skip_edit macro data tool.

*Section 2:* Special formats are created using the word SKIP to identify values that will trigger skipping a variable.

*Section 3:* Macro variables (&original_data and &edit_data) are initialized with the names of the original data and a name for the final version of the edited data set. Ensuring that the original data has an unchanged copy is an important part of your SAS program because there is no guarantee that everything will be done right during data cleaning and preparation activities. It should always be possible to repeat all steps of data preparation starting from the original data. A temporary version (edit) of the SAS data set (&original_data) is created for use by the %TK_skip_edit macro program. %TK_skip_edit will edit this data set as needed to repair inconsistent flow through skip patterns. Every time the %TK_skip_edit program is invoked, one variable will have its values examined and, if needed, edited to provide a consistent flow through the skip pattern. The name of the temporary version of the data is stored in the variable &edit_data. The data is overwritten every time %TK_skip_edit is invoked. When a variable is being checked (CHECK_VAR) the values of the skip variables (SKIP_VARS) might be the edited values if they were the CHECK_VAR in a previous invocation of %TK_SKIP_EDIT in this SAS job.

*Section 4:* SAS statements in this section use ODS to open a file with the RTF destination to write results from evaluating the flow of each variable through prescribed skip patterns. Except for the invocation where the skip pattern for variable PG3 was being examined for version 1 observations, all executions of %TK_skip_edit use default values for the optional keyword parameters (Legit_Skip=.L, Expect_Reply=.E, print_xtab=YES, tally_edits=YES). The survey questions displayed in Survey 7-1c show that question PG3 was added in the second version of the survey. Since this question was not available for women who were interviewed with the first version of the survey the default value of .L is replaced with .N as shown in the following statement:

```
%TK_skip_edit(check_var = PG3,
            skip_vars = VERSION,
            skip_fmts = VERSION skip1f.,
```

```
        SUBGROUP= Version=1,
        legit_skip=.N);
```

This statement will also use .N for males filling out version 1 of the survey even though they would not have been asked the pregnancy questions.

*Section 5:* Next, %TK_skip_edit uses ODS to save a copy of the tally report showing the number of edits for each variable that were needed to correct the data flowing through each skip pattern. PROC DATASETS removes the tally data sets created for the tally report. Since %TK_skip_edit appends to the tally set, this ensures a new tally data set will be created if this program is run multiple times in the same session.

*Section 6:* The last step is to save the edited version of the data set as a permanent SAS data set.

**Program 7-3: Check and Edit Data with Skip Patterns**

```
title "Program7_3_Skip_Edit: Check Skip Path & Edit when necessary to
correct flow through skip pattern";
options nocenter noreplace nofmterr symbolgen mprint;
options papersize=letter orientation=portrait leftmargin=1.0in
rightmargin=1.0in topmargin=1.5in bottommargin=1.5in;

/* Section 1) Define folders, library references for data, and include
   TK_skip_edit.sas macro program*/
%let TKFolder = /Data_Detective/Book/SAS_programs/TK_toolkit;
%let DataFolder = /Data_Detective/Book/SAS_Datasets;
%let WorkFolder = /Data_Detective/Book/SAS_Output;
libname SAS_out "&WorkFolder";
libname SAS_data "&DataFolder";

%include "&TKFolder./TK_skip_edit.sas";

/* Section 2) Create special skip formats used by the TK_skip_recode.sas
   macro*/
proc format;
   value SKIP0f 0='0=SKIP';
   value SKIP1f 1='1=SKIP';
   value SKIP2f 2='2=SKIP';
   value SKIP3f 3='3=SKIP';
   value SKIP1_2f 1='1=SKIP' 2='2=SKIP';
   value SKIP2_3f 2='2=SKIP' 3='3=SKIP';
   value SKIP3_4f 3='3=SKIP' 4='4=SKIP';
   value TOB2SKIP 0='0=SKIP' 1-30 = "1-30=ask";
   value svy_mode 1="Web" 2="Mail";

run;

/* Section 3) Define macro variables for original and edited data sets
   and make copy of original data for TK_skip macro to edit.*/
/* The TK_skip_edit macro will overwrite this data set with edited values
   as needed while leaving the original data untouched.*/
%let original_data = SAS_data.skippatterndata; /* Original data - no
                                                  editing */
%let edit_data = SAS_data.skippatterndata_cln;  /* Data with skip patterns
                                                  validated and edited*/
```

```
/* Make a temporary version of the data set so that the original data set
   is not overwritten.*/
data edit;
   set &original_data(rename=(mode=svy_mode));
run;

/* Create a macro variable with the name of the temporary data set created
   in the previous DATA step.*/
%let output_set = edit;

/* Section 4) Check skip paths & edit to correct incorrect flow through
   skip pattern*/
/* Save crosstabs (created if print_xtab=YES) to check editing results
   in an RTF file */
/* The following RTF file will have the tables shown in Crosstab 7-3 to
Crosstab 7-4 */
ods rtf file="&WorkFolder./Skip_Edit_xtab7_3.rtf" style = rtf bodytitle;
ods noproctitle;

/* Part 1: Demographics - No skips affect demographic variables*/
/* Part 2: Tobacco Use*/
/* If tally_edits=YES, then provide data set name to hold results by
   creating macro variable &tally_results*/
%let tally_results = Part2_tally;

%TK_skip_edit(check_var=TOB2, skip_vars=TOB1, strata_var=svy_mode,
   skip_fmts=TOB1 skip2f. , strata_fmt=svy_mode svy_mode.);
%TK_skip_edit(check_var=TOB3, skip_vars=TOB1, strata_var=svy_mode,
   skip_fmts=TOB1 skip2f. , strata_fmt=svy_mode svy_mode.);
%TK_skip_edit(check_var=TOB4, skip_vars=TOB1, strata_var=svy_mode,
   skip_fmts=TOB1 skip2f. , strata_fmt=svy_mode svy_mode.);
%TK_skip_edit(check_var=TOB5, skip_vars=TOB1*TOB2, strata_var=svy_mode,
skip_fmts=TOB1 skip2f. TOB2 TOB2skip., strata_fmt=svy_mode svy_mode.);

/* Part 3: Pregnancy History*/
/* If tally_edits=YES and you want separate sets for the results, then
   provide data set name*/
/* Create macro variable &tally_results to hold results*/
%let tally_results = Part3_tally;

%TK_skip_edit(check_var=PG1, skip_vars=DEM2, skip_fmts=DEM2 skip2f.,
   strata_fmt=svy_mode svy_mode.);
%TK_skip_edit(check_var=PG2, skip_vars=DEM2*PG1,
   skip_fmts=DEM2 skip2f. PG1 skip2f. , strata_fmt=svy_mode svy_mode.);
%TK_skip_edit(check_var=PG3, skip_vars=VERSION, skip_fmts=VERSION skip1f.,
   SUBGROUP= Version=1, legit_skip=.N, strata_fmt=svy_mode svy_mode.);
%TK_skip_edit(check_var=PG3, skip_vars=VERSION*DEM2*PG1,
   skip_fmts=VERSION skip1f. DEM2 skip2f. PG1 skip2f.,
   SUBGROUP= Version>1, strata_fmt=svy_mode svy_mode.);
%TK_skip_edit(check_var=PG4, skip_vars=DEM2*PG1,
   skip_fmts=DEM2 skip1f. PG1 skip2f. , strata_fmt=svy_mode svy_mode.);
%TK_skip_edit(check_var=PG5, skip_vars=DEM2*PG1*PG4,
   skip_fmts=DEM2 skip2f. PG1 skip2f. PG4 skip2_3f.,
   strata_fmt=svy_mode svy_mode.);
ods rtf close;

/* Section 5) Print tally report showing a summary of the edits done on
   the data*/
```

```
ods escapechar="^";
title1 "Tally Report for Editing original data set: &original_data";
title2 "Final cleaned data set: &edit_data";
footnote1 "Editing Rules for Variables:";
footnote2 "^{super 0}OK: Missing when should be skipped, then edit value =
.L (Legitimate Skip) or .N (Question Not Available)";
footnote3 "^{super 1}OK: Answered when expected reply, then value is
unchanged";
footnote4 "^{super 2}BAD: Answered when should skip, then edit value = .L
(Legitimate Skip)";
footnote5 "^{super 3}BAD: Missing when reply expected, then edit value = .E
(Expected Reply)";
/* The following RTF file will have the tables shown in Crosstab 7-3 to
Crosstab 7-4 */
ods rtf file="&WorkFolder./Skip_Edit_Tally7_3.rtf" style = rtf bodytitle;

proc format;
value TK_status 0="OK^{super 0} ^nKeep ^nOriginal ^nValue"
        1 = "OK^{super 1} ^nLegit Skip ^nRecode"
        2="BAD^{super 2} ^nAnswered, ^nShould Skip"
        3="BAD^{super 3} ^nExpect Reply, ^nNo Answer";
value mode 1="Web" 2="Mail";
run;
proc tabulate data=part2_tally missing;
class check_var skip_status svy_mode subgroup;
var count;
tables (check_var*subgroup=" "),(svy_mode=" "*skip_status all)*COUNT='
'*(SUM=' '*F=6.0)/row=float;
format skip_status TK_status.;
format svy_mode mode.;
run;

proc tabulate data=part3_tally missing;
class check_var skip_status subgroup;
var count;
tables (check_var*subgroup=" "),(skip_status all)*COUNT=" "*(SUM='
'*F=6.0)/row=float;
format skip_status TK_status.;
format svy_mode mode.;
run;

ods rtf close;
/* Remove data sets with results of editing data*/

proc datasets nolist;
   delete Part2_tally Part3_tally;
run;

/* Section 6) Create permanent SAS data set with edited results*/
options replace;

data &edit_data;
   set &output_set;
run;

options noreplace;
```

## Examining the Tally Report

The tally report for the Tobacco variables from Part 2 of the Survey appears in Crosstab 7-3. This report is stratified by variable SVY_MODE and counts the number of edits done to correct inconsistent flow through the skip pattern. The "Editing Rules for Variables" at the bottom of the table briefly explains what edits are included in the counts appearing in each column. Entries in these three columns are derived as followed:

- The "OK" columns include the number of participants for the question who correctly went through the skip path with no problems. This means that the variable had an original value of SAS missing (recoded to .L) or provided a response when expected.

- The "BAD Answered" column includes the number of participants who should have skipped the question but gave a response. These unexpected responses were recoded to the .L special SAS missing value.

- The final column, "BAD Expect Reply" column reports the number of participants who did not answer but were expected to answer. For these variables, the original value of SAS missing was recoded to be the .E special SAS missing value.

Inspecting this synopsis of edits provides an overview of how well the collected data matched the intended skip paths. The edits reported in the "Legitimate Skip" or "Expect Reply" columns indicate possible problems with the implementation of the survey or with the translation of the skip pattern into the %TK_skip_edit statements. For example:

- Two participants provided an answer for TOB2 while five provided answers for TOB5 when they should have skipped past the question.

- Question TOB3 had five Web and two Mail participants fail to answer when they were presented the question.

- Question TOB5 had 19 Web and 20 Mail missing values when TOB5 should have been answered. This is higher than the rest of the variables indicating that the skip path information programmed into the %TK_skip_edit for this variable should be rechecked.

If the skip pattern logic has been expressed correctly in the %TK_skip_edit statement, then further investigation is warranted. Consulting the crosstab created by %TK_skip_edit will provide more detailed information about the editing process for each variable. The programming for web or computerized surveys should be re-checked for logic errors while the printed instructions for teleform or paper surveys should be reviewed. Early implementation and use of the %TK_skip_edit macro is a good way to find programming mistakes or poorly specified skip logic in the survey to be discovered and corrected before the survey is put into the field.

### Crosstab 7-3: Number of Edits for Tobacco Variables
*Tally Report for Editing original data set: SAS_data.skippatterndata*
*Final cleaned data set: SAS_data.skippatterndata_cln*

| | Web | | | | Mail | | | | |
|---|---|---|---|---|---|---|---|---|---|
| | Skip Pattern Edit Status | | | | Skip Pattern Edit Status | | | | |
| | OK[0] Keep Original Value | OK[1] Legit Skip Recode | BAD[2] Answered, Should Skip | BAD[3] Expect Reply, No Answer | OK[0] Keep Original Value | OK[1] Legit Skip Recode | BAD[2] Answered, Should Skip | BAD[3] Expect Reply, No Answer | All |
| **Variable Checked** | | | | | | | | | |
| **TOB2** | 171 | 175 | 2 | . | 171 | 177 | 5 | . | 701 |
| **TOB3** | 166 | 177 | . | 5 | 169 | 182 | . | 2 | 701 |
| **TOB4** | 171 | 177 | . | . | 171 | 182 | . | . | 701 |
| **TOB5** | 148 | 177 | 4 | 19 | 149 | 182 | 2 | 20 | 701 |

*Editing Rules for Variables:*
*[0]OK: Missing when should be skipped, then edit value = .L (Legitimate Skip) or .N (Question Not Available)*
*[1]OK: Answered when expected reply, then value is unchanged*
*[2]BAD: Answered when should skip, then edit value = .L (Legitimate Skip)*
*[3]BAD: Missing when reply expected, then edit value = .E (Expected Reply)*

The tally report for the Pregnancy variables in Part 3 of the survey show four questions were answered by a few participants when they should have not been asked the question:

- PG1 had seven Web and three Mail participants who answered but should have skipped
- PG2 had one Web and one Mail participants who answered but should have skipped
- PG3 had one Web and one Mail participants who answered but should have skipped
- PG4 had one Web and one Mail participants who answered but should have skipped
- None of the pregnancy questions were left blank when the participant was expected to provide an answer

## Crosstab 7-4: Number of Edits for Pregnancy Variables

*Tally Report for Editing original data set: SAS_data.skippatterndata*
*Final cleaned data set: SAS_data.skippatterndata_cln*

| | | Web | | | Mail | | | |
| --- | --- | --- | --- | --- | --- | --- | --- | --- |
| | | Skip Pattern Edit Status | | | Skip Pattern Edit Status | | | |
| | | OK[0] Keep Original Value | OK[1] Legit Skip Recode | BAD[2] Answered, Should Skip | OK[0] Keep Original Value | OK[1] Legit Skip Recode | BAD[2] Answered, Should Skip | All |
| **Variable Checked** | | | | | | | | |
| PG1 | | 177 | 164 | 7 | 154 | 196 | 3 | 701 |
| PG2 | | 87 | 260 | 1 | 72 | 280 | 1 | 701 |
| PG3 | Version=1 | . | 79 | . | . | 70 | . | 149 |
| | Version>1 | 68 | 200 | 1 | 59 | 223 | 1 | 552 |
| PG4 | | 87 | 260 | 1 | 72 | 280 | 1 | 701 |
| PG5 | | 24 | 324 | . | 17 | 336 | . | 701 |

*Editing Rules for Variables:*
*[0]OK: Missing when should be skipped, then edit value = .L (Legitimate Skip) or .N (Question Not Available)*
*[1]OK: Answered when expected reply, then value is unchanged*
*[2]BAD: Answered when should skip, then edit value = .L (Legitimate Skip)*
*[3]BAD: Missing when reply expected, then edit value = .E (Expected Reply)*

## Examining the Edits Reported in the Crosstab Tables

The next step is to examine the crosstab tables created to display the flow of variables through the skip pattern and editing of the values to ensure a consistent flow. Any large or unexpected number of edits in the table should be carefully examined with the following actions:

- Examine the questions in the survey to see whether you need to correct the list of skip variables specified in the %TK_skip_edit statement and run again.

- Print observations for incorrect paths to investigate how the survey was implemented. The variables printed should include the unique record identifier, values of the variable being checked, skip variables, and subgroup.

  - For teleform or paper surveys, give this printout to the person who developed the survey. This helps them understand how the participant interpreted the written survey and helps identify confusing wording in the instructions on skipping questions.

  - For web or computer-based surveys, give this printout to the programmer who developed the automated survey. This guides them in reviewing the part of their source code controlling the path a participant with inconsistent data followed.

Examining the crosstab tables with data created by testing of the survey with hypothetical participants or with a pilot survey enables you to make improvements in implementation or design of the survey before mistakes become problems in the data.

## TOB2 Results

Crosstab 7-5 shows the following:

- 2=BAD: Variable TOB2 had incorrect flow through the skip pattern for five Mail and two Web participants out of the 701 participants.

    ○ These seven participants were non-smokers (TOB1=2) who answered TOB2 "How many of the past 30 days did you smoke?" Because these participants were non-smokers, they should have skipped question TOB2.

    ○ The data for these participants was edited to replace their responses (11,13,18, 22) to .L to indicate Legitimate Skip.

- The remaining 696 participants had no problems with the skip pattern.

    ○ 1=OK: For 352 of these participants (175 Web and 177 Mail) who had never smoked (TOB1=2) the value of TOB2 = . (SAS default missing value) was edited to .L to indicate Legitimate Skip.

    ○ O=OK: No change was made to the original value of TOB2 for the participants who reported smoking cigarettes, even just one or two puffs (TOB1=1).

## Crosstab 7-5: TOB2 Edited with %*TK_skip_edit*

*Checking: TOB2 with skip variables: TOB1, skip formats: TOB1 skip2f.*

| TOB2: Edits correcting flow through Skip Pattern for all observations | | | | svy_mode | | |
| | | | | Web | Mail | Count |
| | | | | N | N | N |
| Type of Edit Performed | Recoded TOB2 | Original TOB2 | TOB1 | | | |
| 0=OK: Keep Original Value | 0 | 0 | 1 | 4 | 2 | 6 |
| | 1 | 1 | 1 | 5 | 5 | 10 |
| | 2 | 2 | 1 | 4 | 7 | 11 |
| | 3 | 3 | 1 | 4 | 6 | 10 |
| | 4 | 4 | 1 | 3 | 6 | 9 |
| | 5 | 5 | 1 | 11 | 5 | 16 |
| | 6 | 6 | 1 | 6 | 9 | 15 |
| | 7 | 7 | 1 | 5 | 6 | 11 |
| | 8 | 8 | 1 | 6 | 3 | 9 |

| TOB2: Edits correcting flow through Skip Pattern for all observations | | | svy_mode | | |
|---|---|---|---|---|---|
| | | | Web | Mail | Count |
| | | | N | N | N |
| 9 | 9 | 1 | 3 | 5 | 8 |
| 10 | 10 | 1 | 6 | 6 | 12 |
| 11 | 11 | 1 | 5 | . | 5 |
| 12 | 12 | 1 | 5 | 5 | 10 |
| 13 | 13 | 1 | 2 | 8 | 10 |
| 14 | 14 | 1 | 7 | 5 | 12 |
| 15 | 15 | 1 | 7 | 8 | 15 |
| 16 | 16 | 1 | 8 | 6 | 14 |
| 17 | 17 | 1 | 6 | 3 | 9 |
| 18 | 18 | 1 | 2 | 8 | 10 |
| 19 | 19 | 1 | 4 | 6 | 10 |
| 20 | 20 | 1 | 6 | 4 | 10 |
| 21 | 21 | 1 | 3 | 6 | 9 |
| 22 | 22 | 1 | 7 | 7 | 14 |
| 23 | 23 | 1 | 4 | 6 | 10 |
| 24 | 24 | 1 | 4 | 5 | 9 |
| 25 | 25 | 1 | 10 | 7 | 17 |
| 26 | 26 | 1 | 3 | 9 | 12 |
| 27 | 27 | 1 | 8 | 8 | 16 |
| 28 | 28 | 1 | 10 | 3 | 13 |
| 29 | 29 | 1 | 7 | 4 | 11 |
| 30 | 30 | 1 | 6 | 3 | 9 |
| 1=OK: Legitimate Skip Recode SAS missing to .L | L | . | 2=SKIP | 175 | 177 | 352 |
| 2=BAD: Answered, Should Skip: Recode to .L | L | 1 | 2=SKIP | 1 | . | 1 |
| | | 6 | 2=SKIP | . | 1 | 1 |
| | | 10 | 2=SKIP | . | 1 | 1 |
| | | 15 | 2=SKIP | . | 1 | 1 |
| | | 16 | 2=SKIP | . | 1 | 1 |

| TOB2: Edits correcting flow through Skip Pattern for all observations | | | | svy_mode | | |
|---|---|---|---|---|---|---|
| | | | | Web | Mail | Count |
| | | | | N | N | N |
| | | 22 | 2=SKIP | 1 | . | 1 |
| | | 25 | 2=SKIP | . | 1 | 1 |
| Total Observations | | | | 348 | 353 | 701 |

## TOB3 Results

Crosstab 7-6 (3=BAD) shows the flow through the skip pattern TOB3 has five Web and two Mail participants who were smokers (TOB1=1) failed to answer TOB3 "Have you smoked at least 100 cigarettes in your entire life?" For these participants the original value of default SAS missing (.) was recoded to .E indicating Expect Reply.

**Crosstab 7-6: TOB3 Edited with %TK_skip_edit**

*Checking: TOB3 with skip variables: TOB1, skip formats: TOB1 skip2f.*

| TOB3: Edits correcting flow through Skip Pattern for all observations | | | | svy_mode | | |
|---|---|---|---|---|---|---|
| | | | | Web | Mail | Count |
| | | | | N | N | N |
| Type of Edit Performed | Recoded TOB3 | Original TOB3 | TOB1 | | | |
| 0=OK: Keep Original Value | 1 | 1 | 1 | 83 | 83 | 166 |
| | 2 | 2 | 1 | 83 | 86 | 169 |
| 1=OK: Legitimate Skip Recode SAS missing to .L | L | . | 2=SKIP | 177 | 182 | 359 |
| 3=BAD: Expect Reply, No Answer: Recode to .E | E | . | 1 | 5 | 2 | 7 |
| Total Observations | | | | 348 | 353 | 701 |

## TOB4 Results

No issues were found with TOB4 flow through the skip pattern. All values remained unchanged.

## Crosstab 7-7: TOB4 Edited with %TK_skip_edit

*Checking: TOB4 with skip variables: TOB1, skip formats: TOB1 skip2f.*

| TOB4: Edits correcting flow through Skip Pattern for all observations | | | | svy_mode | | |
|---|---|---|---|---|---|---|
| | | | | Web | Mail | Count |
| | | | | N | N | N |
| **Type of Edit Performed** | **Recoded TOB4** | **Original TOB4** | **TOB1** | | | |
| **0=OK:** Keep Original Value | 1 | 1 | 1 | 91 | 99 | 190 |
| | 2 | 2 | 1 | 80 | 72 | 152 |
| **1=OK:** Legitimate Skip Recode SAS missing to .L | L | . | 2=SKIP | 177 | 182 | 359 |
| **Total Observations** | | | | 348 | 353 | 701 |

## TOB5 Results

Examining the Crosstab 7-8 shows the following edits to correct flow through the skip pattern:

- 2=BAD: Four Web and two Mail participants did not smoke in the past 30 days (TOB2=0) answered TOB5 when they should have skipped TOB5.
    - These six participants original_values of TOB5 were edited to .L indicating Legitimate Skip.

- 3=BAD: Nineteen Web and 20 Mail participants did not answer TOB5 when they were expected to answer (TOB1=1 indicating ever smoked, 1<=TOB2<=30 indicating smoked during the last 30 days).
    - These 39 participants original value of SAS missing (.) were recoded to .E to indicate a reply was expected but no answer was given.

- 1=OK: No issues were found with the flow of data through the skip pattern for the following participants.
    - There were 359 of 701 who skipped question TOB5 because they were nonsmokers (TOB1=2).
    - These 359 participants had the SAS missing value (.) recoded to be .L indicating Legitimate Skip.

- 0=OK: The remaining participants provided an answer to TOB5 when expected; no change was made to their data values.

## Crosstab 7-8: TOB5 Edited with %*TK_skip_edit*

*Checking: TOB5 with skip variables: TOB1\*TOB2, skip formats: TOB1 skip2f. TOB2 TOB2skip.*

| TOB5: Edits correcting flow through Skip Pattern for all observations | | | | | svy_mode | | |
|---|---|---|---|---|---|---|---|
| | | | | | Web | Mail | Count |
| | | | | | N | N | N |
| **Type of Edit Performed** | Recoded TOB5 | Original TOB5 | TOB1 | TOB2 | | | |
| **0=OK:** **Keep Original Value** | 1 | 1 | 1 | 1-30=ask | 87 | 88 | 175 |
| | 2 | 2 | 1 | 1-30=ask | 42 | 33 | 75 |
| | 3 | 3 | 1 | 1-30=ask | 9 | 14 | 23 |
| | 4 | 4 | 1 | 1-30=ask | 10 | 14 | 24 |
| **1=OK:** **Legitimate Skip** **Recode SAS missing to .L** | L | . | 2=SKIP | L | 177 | 182 | 359 |
| **2=BAD: Answered, Should Skip:** **Recode to .L** | L | 1 | 1 | 0=SKIP | 1 | 2 | 3 |
| | | 2 | 1 | 0=SKIP | 2 | . | 2 |
| | | 4 | 1 | 0=SKIP | 1 | . | 1 |
| **3=BAD: Expect Reply, No Answer:** **Recode to .E** | E | . | 1 | 1-30=ask | 19 | 20 | 39 |
| **Total Observations** | | | | | 348 | 353 | 701 |

## PG1 Results

Crosstab 7-9 (2=BAD) shows that there were 10 males (DEM2=2) who answered question PG1 "Have you ever been pregnant?" These answers were edited to be .L for legitimate skip. The remaining 691 participants flowed through the skip path correctly. The SAS missing value (.) was edited to be .L for 360 male participants (DEM2=1). No other editing was need for PG1.

## Crosstab 7-9: PG1 Edited with %*TK_skip_edit*

*Checking: PG1 with skip variables: DEM2, skip formats: DEM2 skip2f.*

| PG1: Edits correcting flow through Skip Pattern for all observations | | | | svy_mode | | |
|---|---|---|---|---|---|---|
| | | | | Web | Mail | Count |
| | | | | N | N | N |
| **Type of Edit Performed** | Recoded PG1 | Original PG1 | DEM2 | | | |
| | 1 | 1 | 1 | 87 | 72 | 159 |

| PG1: Edits correcting flow through Skip Pattern for all observations | | | | svy_mode | | |
|---|---|---|---|---|---|---|
| | | | | Web | Mail | Count |
| | | | | N | N | N |
| 0=OK: Keep Original Value | 2 | 2 | 1 | 90 | 82 | 172 |
| 1=OK: Legitimate Skip Recode SAS missing to .L | L | . | 2=SKIP | 164 | 196 | 360 |
| 2=BAD: Answered, Should Skip: Recode to .L | L | 1 | 2=SKIP | 4 | 3 | 7 |
| | | 2 | 2=SKIP | 3 | . | 3 |
| Total Observations | | | | 348 | 353 | 701 |

## PG2 Results

Crosstab 7-10 shows the editing process for variable PG2. One Web and one Mail participant (2=BAD) reported no pregnancies (PG1=2) but have an answer for PG2 "How many pregnancies have you had?" These responses were recoded to Legitimate Skips (.L). The remaining participants had correct flow through the skip pattern.

### Crosstab 7-10: PG2 Edited with %*TK_skip_edit*
*Checking: PG2 with skip variables: DEM2\*PG1, skip formats: DEM2 skip2f. PG1 skip2f.*

| PG2: Edits correcting flow through Skip Pattern for all observations | | | | | svy_mode | | |
|---|---|---|---|---|---|---|---|
| | | | | | Web | Mail | Count |
| | | | | | N | N | N |
| Type of Edit Performed | Recoded PG2 | Original PG2 | DEM2 | PG1 | | | |
| 0=OK: Keep Original Value | 1 | 1 | 1 | 1 | 4 | 4 | 8 |
| | 2 | 2 | 1 | 1 | 11 | 9 | 20 |
| | 3 | 3 | 1 | 1 | 9 | 4 | 13 |
| | 4 | 4 | 1 | 1 | 7 | 8 | 15 |
| | 5 | 5 | 1 | 1 | 6 | 8 | 14 |
| | 6 | 6 | 1 | 1 | 11 | 7 | 18 |
| | 7 | 7 | 1 | 1 | 10 | 10 | 20 |
| | 8 | 8 | 1 | 1 | 10 | 3 | 13 |
| | 9 | 9 | 1 | 1 | 12 | 13 | 25 |
| | 10 | 10 | 1 | 1 | 7 | 6 | 13 |

| PG2: Edits correcting flow through Skip Pattern for all observations | | | | | svy_mode | | |
|---|---|---|---|---|---|---|---|
| | | | | | Web | Mail | Count |
| | | | | | N | N | N |
| 1=OK: Legitimate Skip Recode SAS missing to .L | L | . | 1 | 2=SKIP | 89 | 81 | 170 |
| | | | 2=SKIP | L | 171 | 199 | 370 |
| 2=BAD: Answered, Should Skip: Recode to .L | L | 5 | 1 | 2=SKIP | 1 | . | 1 |
| | 8 | 1 | 2=SKIP | | . | 1 | 1 |
| Total Observations | | | | | 348 | 353 | 701 |

## PG3 Results

Question PG3 was added to version 2 of the survey. Note the crosstab is subset to only display the participants who took version 1 of the survey. As shown in Crosstab 7-11, everyone who was given version 1 of the survey has variable PG3 edited from SAS missing value (.) to = .N to indicate the question was "Not Available" when the participant filled out the survey. This coding helps scientists using the data decide the best way to handle missing data.

### Crosstab 7-11: PG3 (Version 1) Edited with %*TK_skip_edit*

*Checking: PG3 with skip variables: VERSION, skip formats: VERSION skip1f.*

| PG3: Edits correcting flow through Skip Pattern for data subset to Version=1 | | | | svy_mode | | |
|---|---|---|---|---|---|---|
| | | | | Web | Mail | Count |
| | | | | N | N | N |
| Type of Edit Performed | Recoded PG3 | Original PG3 | VERSION | | | |
| 1=OK: Legitimate Skip Recode SAS missing to .N | N | . | 1=SKIP | 79 | 70 | 149 |
| Total Observations | | | | 79 | 70 | 149 |

Crosstab 7-12 shows the editing process for question PG3 subset to participants who received version 2 or later of the survey.

The results are as follows:

- 2=BAD: Only two participants (one Web, one Mail) who never had been pregnant (PG1=2) and should have skipped PG3 reported pregnancies. The values of PG3 were edited to .L (Legitimate Skip) for these women.

- 1=OK: The 136+287=423 women who correctly skipped question PG3 have their SAS missing value (.) edited to .L.

- 0=OK: No other editing was done for the remaining participants.

## Crosstab 7-12: PG3 ((Version>1) Edited with %*TK_skip_edit*

*Checking: PG3 with skip variables: VERSION\*DEM2\*PG1, skip formats: VERSION skip1f. DEM2 skip2f. PG1 skip2f.*

| | | | | | | svy_mode | | |
|---|---|---|---|---|---|---|---|---|
| PG3: Edits correcting flow through Skip Pattern for data subset to Version>1 | | | | | | Web | Mail | Count |
| | | | | | | N | N | N |
| Type of Edit Performed | Recoded PG3 | Original PG3 | VERSION | DEM2 | PG1 | | | |
| 0=OK:<br>Keep Original Value | 1 | 1 | 2 | 1 | 1 | 3 | 2 | 5 |
| | 2 | 2 | 2 | 1 | 1 | 5 | 7 | 12 |
| | 3 | 3 | 2 | 1 | 1 | 8 | 8 | 16 |
| | 4 | 4 | 2 | 1 | 1 | 6 | 4 | 10 |
| | 5 | 5 | 2 | 1 | 1 | 11 | 6 | 17 |
| | 6 | 6 | 2 | 1 | 1 | 11 | 9 | 20 |
| | 7 | 7 | 2 | 1 | 1 | 7 | 11 | 18 |
| | 8 | 8 | 2 | 1 | 1 | 5 | 3 | 8 |
| | 9 | 9 | 2 | 1 | 1 | 10 | 7 | 17 |
| | 10 | 10 | 2 | 1 | 1 | 2 | 2 | 4 |
| 1=OK:<br>Legitimate Skip<br>Recode SAS missing to .L | L | . | 2 | 1 | 2=SKIP | 69 | 67 | 136 |
| | | | | 2=SKIP | L | 131 | 156 | 287 |
| 2=BAD: Answered, Should Skip:<br>Recode to .L | L | 7 | 2 | 1 | 2=SKIP | . | 1 | 1 |
| | 9 | 2 | 1 | 2=SKIP | 1 | . | 1 |
| Total Observations | | | | | | 269 | 283 | 552 |

## PG4 Results

Crosstab 7-13 shows the following:

- 2=BAD: One Web and one Mail woman (DEM2=1) reporting never pregnant (PG1=2) answered PG4 when they should have skipped the question. The values of PG4 for these women were recoded to .L indicating Legitimate Skip.

- 1=OK: Of the remaining women, 170+370 = 540 correctly skipped question PG4 causing their value of PG4 to be recoded to .L indicating Legitimate Skip.

- 0=OK: No other recoding was done for the remaining 168 women.

## Crosstab 7-13: PG4 Edited with %*TK_skip_edit*

*Checking: PG4 with skip variables: DEM2\*PG1, skip formats: DEM2 skip2f. PG1 skip2f.*

| PG4: Edits correcting flow through Skip Pattern for all observations | | | | | svy_mode | | |
|---|---|---|---|---|---|---|---|
| | | | | | Web | Mail | Count |
| | | | | | N | N | N |
| **Type of Edit Performed** | Recoded PG4 | Original PG4 | DEM2 | PG1 | | | |
| **0=OK:** Keep Original Value | 1 | 1 | 1 | 1 | 24 | 17 | 41 |
| | 2 | 2 | 1 | 1 | 43 | 36 | 79 |
| | 3 | 3 | 1 | 1 | 20 | 19 | 39 |
| **1=OK:** Legitimate Skip Recode SAS missing to .L | L | . | 1 | 2=SKIP | 89 | 81 | 170 |
| | | | 2=SKIP | L | 171 | 199 | 370 |
| **2=BAD: Answered, Should Skip:** Recode to .L | L | 1 | 1 | 2=SKIP | 1 | . | 1 |
| | | 2 | ◊1 | 2=SKIP | . | 1 | 1 |
| **Total Observations** | | | | | 348 | 353 | 701 |

## PG5 Results

Crosstab 7-14 shows that all participants have PG5 response values consistent with the skip pattern.

## Crosstab 7-14: PG5 Edited with %*TK_skip_edit*

*Checking: PG5 with skip variables: DEM2\*PG1\*PG4, skip formats: DEM2 skip2f. PG1 skip2f. PG4 skip2_3f.*

| PG5: Edits correcting flow through Skip Pattern for all observations | | | | | | svy_mode | | |
|---|---|---|---|---|---|---|---|---|
| | | | | | | Web | Mail | Count |
| | | | | | | N | N | N |
| **Type of Edit Performed** | Recoded PG5 | Original PG5 | DEM2 | PG1 | PG4 | | | |
| **0=OK:** Keep Original Value | 1 | 1 | 1 | 1 | 1 | 2 | 1 | 3 |
| | 2 | 2 | 1 | 1 | 1 | 5 | 3 | 8 |
| | 3 | 3 | 1 | 1 | 1 | . | 2 | 2 |
| | 4 | 4 | 1 | 1 | 1 | 3 | 2 | 5 |
| | 5 | 5 | 1 | 1 | 1 | 2 | 2 | 4 |
| | 6 | 6 | 1 | 1 | 1 | 5 | 3 | 8 |

| PG5: Edits correcting flow through Skip Pattern for all observations | | | | | | svy_mode | | |
|---|---|---|---|---|---|---|---|---|
| | | | | | | Web | Mail | Count |
| | | | | | | N | N | N |
| | 7 | 7 | 1 | 1 | 1 | 2 | 1 | 3 |
| | 8 | 8 | 1 | 1 | 1 | 4 | 2 | 6 |
| | 9 | 9 | 1 | 1 | 1 | 1 | 1 | 2 |
| 1=OK: Legitimate Skip Recode SAS missing to .L | L | . | 1 | 1 | 2=SKIP | 43 | 36 | 79 |
| | | | | | 3=SKIP | 20 | 19 | 39 |
| | | | | 2=SKIP | L | 90 | 82 | 172 |
| | | | 2=SKIP | L | L | 171 | 199 | 370 |
| Total Observations | | | | | | 348 | 353 | 701 |

Appendix B contains a codebook for the skip pattern data set after all skip patterns have been examined and values edited as needed.

# Inside the Toolkit: How %TK_skip_edit Works

The source code for the %TK_skip_edit macro is more involved than other macros available in the *Data Detective's Toolkit*. Although changing the logic for editing the inconsistent values would require some careful thought, there is one modification that you might want to make for your project data and it would be quite easy. If you need different codes used for Legitimate Skip (.L) and Expect Reply (.E) you just need to change those values in the statement that begins the macro program. Below is the statement that begins the macro program:

```
%macro TK_skip_edit( check_var=,  skip_vars=, skip_fmts=, subgroup=,
strata_var=,strata_fmt =, Legit_Skip=.L, Expect_Reply=.E, print_xtab=YES,
tally_edits=YES);
```

The %macro TK_skip_edit statement defines eight keyword parameters with four of those parameters having default values used in the process of inspecting data flow through the skip pattern and editing inconsistent values. You can change any of those parameters so that you do not need to include them on the %TK_skip_edit statement. For example, if you know that the numeric variables will never have values of -998 or less, then you can change these parameters:

```
        Legit_Skip=.L, Expect_Reply=.E,
```

To be equal to the values needed for your data set:

```
        Legit_Skip-999, Expect_Reply=-998,
```

The %MACRO statement %TK_skip_edit statement would now be:

```
%macro TK_skip_edit( check_var=,  skip_vars=, skip_fmts=, subgroup=,
strata_var=,strata_fmt =, Legit_Skip=-999, Expect_Reply=-998,
print_xtab=YES, tally_edits=YES);
```

With this change, every time you check a numeric variable that is identified as inconsistent with the flow of the skip pattern, values of -999 and -998 will be used in the editing process. Editing for the character variables would remain unchanged with a blank (' ') used to replace for a text response when the character variable should have been skipped.

Similarly, you can change the YES value for the keyword parameters print_xtab= and tally_edits= to have a value of NO to omit the crosstab output and tally data sets created.

The rest of this section investigates the SAS code in the %TK_skip_edit macro to help you understand how it works. This section is optional but will help you understand how to modify the %TK_skip_edit macro program if you need to customize it for your project data.

### Program 7-4a: Default Values for Parameters and Status Formats

```
%macro TK_skip_edit( check_var=,  skip_vars=, skip_fmts=, subgroup=,
strata_var=,strata_fmt =, Legit_Skip=.L, Expect_Reply=.E, print_xtab=YES,
tally_edits=YES);
    proc format;
        value TK_status 0="0=OK: ^nKeep Original Value"
            1 = "1=OK: ^nLegitimate Skip ^nRecode SAS missing to &Legit_Skip"
            2 = "2=BAD: Answered, Should Skip: ^nRecode to &Legit_Skip"
            3 = "3=BAD: Expect Reply, No Answer: ^nRecode to &Expect_Reply";
    run;
```

Formats are created to help annotate the crosstab reports. Before these formats are used, the ODS ESCAPECHAR statement is used to define ^ to be a special code that SAS interprets as formatting in the output report. The ^n means to start a new line.

%TK_skip_edit needs to know whether the variable being checked is numeric or character.

The macro variable &_tk_and is created as a null variable and will be filled with a value later if the subgroup was specified at the time %TK_skip_edit was used.

The next DATA step creates a macro variable (&CheckVarType) with information about the data type of the variable being checked.

Next, the macro variable &_tk_and is set to the Boolean logic operator AND if the subgroup parameter was given a value when %TK_skip_edit was used. A macro variable is also created with text that can be used in the output report when the crosstab reports are created.

### Program 7-4b: Create Macro Variables to Guide Editing Process

```
%* Determine if check_var is numeric or character;
proc contents data=&output_set(keep=&check_var)
   out=_vartype_(keep=name type) noprint;
run;
%let _tk_and=;
data _null_;
   set _vartype_;
```

```
        /* type: 1 = numeric, 2 = character*/
        if type=1 then
            call symputx("CheckVarType",1);
        else if type=2 then
            call symputx("CheckVarType",2);
        if "&subgroup" ^= "" then do;
            call symputx("_tk_and", "and");
            call symputx("subgroup_text", "for data subset to &subgroup");
            end;
        else do;
            call symputx("subgroup_text", "for all observations");
            end;
    run;
```

The next DATA step initializes the variables used to capture information about the skip variables used in inspecting the skip pattern.

**Program 7-4c: Initialize Variables to Capture Information to Inspect the Skip Pattern**

```
    data &output_set;
        set &output_set;

        /*Number of skip variables that control skipping*/
        _tk_num_checks=0;

        /**Number of skip variables that indicate question should be
            skipped*/
        _tk_num_skips=0;

        /*Number of skip variables with missing values;*/
        _tk_miss_skips=0;
    run;
```

The %DO statement examines the list of skip variables and assigned skip formats, extracting the name of a skip variable and the format with the SKIP values defined. This information is used to go through the data set being edited and collect information about:

- The number of SKIP variables affecting CHECKVAR
- The number of times a SKIP variable has a value causing CHECKVAR to be skipped
- The number of times the SKIP variable has a missing value

The %DO processes every SKIP variable specified in the SKIP_FMTS= parameter, reading through the data set being edited (&OUTPUT_SET) each time.

**Program 7-4d: Determine Flow through Survey from Values of Skip Variables**

```
    /* Tally all skip variables; */
    %do i=1 %to %sysfunc(countw("&skip_fmts"," ")) %by 2;
        %let next_name = %scan(&skip_fmts, &i, %str( ));
        %let next_fmt = %scan(&skip_fmts, &i+1, %str( ));

        data &output_set;
            set &output_set;
```

```
        /*Number of skip variables that control skipping*/
        _tk_num_checks= sum(_tk_num_checks,1);

    if upcase(scan(put(&next_name,&next_fmt),2,'='))="SKIP" then
        do;
            _tk_num_skips = _tk_num_skips+1;
        end;

    if missing(&next_name) then
        _tk_miss_skips=_tk_miss_skips + 1;
run;

%end;
```

The inspection and editing of the &OUTPUT_SET is done in the next DATA step.

The &_TK_AND macro variable has a value only if the &SUBGROUP parameter had a mathematical expression provided for restricting the data set to specific observations for the skip pattern inspection and editing process. If no value was provided, then both of these macro variables have a null value and the resolution of the next statement is "if 1=1 then do;" which is always true. Comments in the source code explain the logic for and editing of the CHECKVAR value that is necessary to correct inconsistent flow through the skip pattern.

**Program 7-4e: Determine Status of Flow through Skip Pattern for Variable Being Checked**

```
    data &output_set;
        set &output_set;
        _ORIGINAL_VALUE_ = &check_var;
        _STATUS_=0;
        if 1=1 &_tk_and &subgroup then
            do;
                /*Numeric*/
                if "&CheckVarType" = "1" then
                    do;
                        /* Incorrect -- Variable being checked should have been
                           skipped;*/
                        if not missing(&check_var) and _tk_num_skips > 0 then
                            do;
                                _status_=1;
                                &check_var=&Legit_Skip;
                            end;

                        /* Incorrect -- Reply expected, but missing; */
                        else if missing(&check_var) and _tk_num_skips=0 and
                            (_tk_miss_skips < _tk_num_checks) then
                            do;
                                _status_=2;
                                &check_var=&Expect_Reply;
                            end;

                        /* Correct -- Variable being checked should have been
                           skipped & was skipped - change SAS missing to
                           &Legit_Skip */
                        /* Leave _status_=0 */
                        if  missing(&check_var) and _tk_num_skips > 0 then
                            do;
```

```
                                &check_var=&Legit_Skip;
                         end;
                 end;

             /*Character*/
             else if "&CheckVarType" = "2"  then
                 do;
                     /* Incorrect -- Variable being checked should have been
                         skipped;*/
                     if not missing(&check_var) and _tk_num_skips > 0 then
                         do;
                             _status_=1;
                             &check_var=" ";
                         end;

                     /* Incorrect -- Reply expected, but not answered; */
                     else if missing(&check_var) and _tk_num_skips=0 and
                       (_tk_miss_skips < _tk_num_checks) then
                         do;
                             _status_=2;
                         end;
                 end;
         end;
   run;
```

The crosstab table, if requested, will be printed next with PROC TABULATE. Note that a TITLE3 statement is used, which will overwrite any previous TITLE statements TITLE3 through TITLE10.

Presence of a value for the &SUBGROUP macro variable adds a statement to restrict the data to only those observations that were being inspected for inconsistent flow through the skip pattern. An informative title is also printed.

**Program 7-4f: Print Crosstab Tables Summarizing Status of Flow Through Skip Pattern**

```
    %if %UPCASE("&print_xtab") = "YES" %then
        %do;
            proc tabulate data=&output_set missing;
            title3 "Checking: &Check_var with skip variables: &skip_vars, skip
formats: &skip_fmts";
                ods escapechar='^';

                %if "&subgroup" ^= "" %then
                    %do;
                        where &subgroup;
                    %end;

                class _all_;
                %if "&strata_var" ^= "" %then %do;
                    tables _status_*&check_var*_original_value_*&skip_vars
                        all= "Total Observations",&strata_var ALL = "Count"
                        /rts=15 row=FLOAT
                        box="&check_var: Edits correcting flow through ^nSkip
Pattern &subgroup_text";
                    %end;
                %else %do;
                    tables _status_*&check_var*_original_value_*&skip_vars
                        all= "Total Observations", ALL = "Count" /rts=15
```

```
                      row=FLOAT box="&check_var: Edits correcting flow through
^nSkip Pattern &subgroup_text";
            %end;
            format _all_;
            format &skip_fmts;
            format _status_ TK_status.;
            %if "&strata_var" ^= "" %then %do;
                label &strata_var = "&strata_var";
                format &strata_var &strata_fmt;
            %end;
            label &check_var = "Recoded ^n &check_var";
            label _original_value_ = "Original ^n &check_var";
            label _status_ = "Type of Edit Performed";
            %do i=1 %to %sysfunc(countw("&skip_fmts"," ")) %by 2;
                %let next_name = %scan(&skip_fmts, &i, ' ');
                label &next_name = "^n &next_name";
            %end;
        run;
title3 ' ';
      %end;
```

If the &TALLY_EDITS parameter is YES, the next part of the macro will add information to the
Tally results file defined in macro variable &TALLY_RESULTS.

**Program 7-4g: Add Summary Information to the Tally Results File**

```
    %if %UPCASE("&tally_edits") = "YES" %then
      %do;

        proc freq data=&output_set noprint;
            %if "&subgroup" ^= "" %then
            %do;
                where &subgroup;
            %end;

        %if "&strata_var" ^= "" %then %do;
            tables _status_*&strata_var /list missing out= _temp_;
        %end;
        %else %do;
        tables _status_ /list missing out= _temp_;
        %end;
      run;
      data _temp_;
      length subgroup $50. check_var $32. skip_vars $50.
         skip_fmts $100. strata_var $32.;
      set _temp_ (drop=percent rename= (_status_=skip_status));
      CHECK_VAR = "&check_var";
      SKIP_VARS = "&skip_vars";
      SKIP_FMTS = "&skip_fmts";
      STRATA_var = "&strata_var";
      SUBGROUP = "&subgroup";
      Legit_Skip = "&Legit_Skip";
      Expect_Reply="&Expect_Reply";
      label skip_status = "Skip Pattern Status";
      label check_var = "Variable Checked";
      label skip_fmts = "Formats Assigned to Skip Variables";
      label skip_vars = "Variables Directing Skip Pattern Flow";
      label skip_status = "Skip Pattern Edit Status";
```

```
       label strata_var = "Strata Variable";
       label subgroup = "Subset of Data Examined";
       label Legit_Skip = "Value used to recode Legitimate Skip";
       label Expect_Reply = "Value used to recode Expect Reply";
       run;

       /* Create the data sets with the results from skip checking and
          recoding */
       %if %sysfunc(exist(&tally_results)) %then
          %do;
             data &tally_results;
                set &tally_results _temp_;  /* _rearrange_;*/
             run;

          %end;
       %else
          %do;
  %put "!!! First set" &Check_var;
             data &tally_results;
                set _temp_;  /*_rearrange_;*/
             run;

          %end;
     %end;
```

The final step is to drop variables from the edited data set &OUTPUT_SET that were created for use by %TK_skip_edit. This ensures the &OUTPUT_SET only has the variables from the original data set.

**Program 7-4h: Drop Temporary Variables from Edited Data Set**

```
   data &output_set;
      set &output_set(drop=_original_value_
        _status_
        _tk_num_skips
        _tk_num_checks
        _tk_miss_skips);
   run;

%mend;
```

# Summary

By using skip patterns to manage the flow of the questions asked, time to administer the survey as well as overall cost can be reduced. Traditional methods of auditing skip paths to identify contradictory responses and incorrect flow of data through a skip path can be very time-consuming when preparing survey data. This chapter has illustrated using the %TK_skip_edit macro to efficiently check the validity of flow through a skip pattern and recode the missing answer to skipped questions to appropriate values.

Advantages of using the %TK_skip_edit to evaluate skip patterns include:

- Reducing programmer's workload

- Increasing data quality by ensuring that consistent rules are used for every skip pattern

- Automatically creating crosstab tables to track the editing process

- Providing summary statistics showing a snapshot of data flow through the skip path for every variable

# Chapter 8: Create and Validate New Variables

## Introduction

Once you have reached this part of the *Data Detective's Toolkit,* your data should be ready for research purposes. Your last step is to enhance the usability of your project data by completing the following programming tasks:

- Adding codes to identify aspects of data quality for each variable

- Creating and validating derived variables

These tasks are the focus of this chapter. Codes that identify aspects of data quality allow users to choose an appropriate analysis method for the data. These codes provide information about why data is missing and can be very useful during variable construction and analysis.

Analysis variables are often the core of why the data set was collected. These variables might be created by research staff and you will be asked to merge them with the collected data. Your job is to cross-check these variables before they are added to the data, ensuring the quality of the data set is maintained. This chapter teaches you some quick ways to do this.

## Coding Variables

Coding techniques are essential for documenting missing values and standardizing text responses into meaningful categories. This book uses the special SAS missing value codes to document the reason a value is missing and to distinguish it from the default SAS missing (.) value code. Doing this has advantages over using numeric codes. Numeric missing value codes would need to be changed to a SAS missing value code for analysis, increasing the work needing to be done by every user of the data. Numeric values must be carefully assigned to avoid assigning a value that can be confused with actual data. However, your project might have established a different convention for the values used when assigning codes. Example 8-1 provides an easy way to recode the SAS missing value codes to numeric values.

## Coding Missing Values

The missing value code conveys important information to the analyst. Codes documenting the reason for missing as "expected reply" or "question not available" provide information about the reason having no answer for the question. These missing value codes provide information useful for using PROC MI to impute a plausible value for these participants.

We used the %TK_skip_edit macro program to code response categories for variables involved in a skip pattern in three categories:

- Legitimate Skip: .L
- Expected Reply: .E
- Question Not Available (Interview 1): .N

Coding missing as a Legitimate Skip (.L) indicates that the data for the participant should be handled in one of two ways. First, questions might not be applicable to the participant. For example, men would be legitimately skipped when asking about a woman's pregnancy history and excluded from any analysis involving this data. Someone who has never smoked in their lifetime would skip questions about the frequency and amount of smoking. Although they would be legitimately skipped from subsequent questions about smoking habits, the analyst would use information from the prior question establishing the participant never smoked. This information would be used to fill in zero for the frequency of smoking and zero for the number of cigarettes smoked. These non-smokers would be included in any analysis about smoking and play an important role as the comparison group to smokers.

Questions can be added, deleted, or modified during the survey. Below are recommendations on using special codes to document these situations:

- Question added in Month/Day/Year or version of survey
  - Participants who did not have question available, edit SAS missing to .N (or code of your choice)
  - Add comment in codebook with date/version question added
- Question dropped in Month/Day/Year or version of survey
  - Participants who did not have question available, edit SAS missing to .D (or code of your choice)
  - Add comment in codebook with date/version question dropped
- Question wording changed in Month/Day/Year or version of survey
  - Add all versions of question to codebook and include date/version wording of question changed.

## Using Formats to Recode Data Values

Not all analysis packages recognize SAS special missing value codes. If you need to distribute your data set to someone using one of these packages, then special SAS missing value codes need to be changed to numeric codes. PROC FORMAT can be used to do this quite easily. This is much simpler than using the IF-THEN-ELSE logic in the DATA step doing the recoding.

## Example 8-1: Using Formats to Recode Data Values

Program 8-1 shows the simple SAS code to use PROC FORMAT to recode a few of the variables from the cleaned skip pattern data set used in the examples in Chapter 7.

**Program 8-1: Using PROC FORMAT to Recode Variables.**

```
* Section 1) Define folders, library references for data.;
%let DataFolder = /Data_Detective/Book/SAS_Datasets;
%let WorkFolder = /Data_Detective/Book/SAS_Output;
libname SAS_out "&WorkFolder";
libname SAS_data "&DataFolder";

*Section 2) Create format used to recode missing data values;

proc format;
   value newcode .L = -97 .N = -99 .E = .;
run;

*Section 3) Use a DATA step to recode the data;

data new(drop=i);
   set SAS_data.skippatterndata_cln;
   array num_vars{*} TOB3 PG3;

   do i=1 to dim(num_vars);
      num_vars(i)=put(num_vars(i), newcode.);
   end;
run;

* Section 4) Merge back with the original data to illustrate how the
recoding worked;

data join;
   merge new (keep=caseid TOB3 PG3)
      SAS_data.skippatterndata_cln(keep=caseid TOB3 PG3
         rename=(TOB3=orig_TOB3 PG3=orig_PG3 ));
   by caseid;
run;

ods rtf file="&WorkFolder./Recode8_1a.rtf" style = statistical bodytitle;
ods noproctitle;

proc freq data=join;
tables TOB3*orig_TOB3 PG3*orig_PG3 /list missing;
run;
ods rtf close;
```

*Section 1:* This section defines the names of folders used in the program and uses the LIBNAME statement to associate a libref with each folder.

*Section 2:* A format is created to associate each SAS special missing value code with a replacement numeric code.

*Section 3:* A DATA step is used to recode two of the variables by using the PUT function to reformat the value or a variable by applying the SAS format.

*Section 4:* To illustrate that the values were updated as desired, a DATA step merges the new and original data values then PROC FREQ creates tables shown in Crosstab 8-1 to compare the new and original values. The special SAS missing values have been recoded with numeric codes.

Crosstab 8-1: Comparison of New and Original Values of Recoded Variables

| TOB3 | orig_TOB3 | Frequency | Percent | Cumulative Frequency | Cumulative Percent |
|------|-----------|-----------|---------|----------------------|--------------------|
| . | E | 7 | 1.00 | 7 | 1.00 |
| -97 | L | 359 | 51.21 | 366 | 52.21 |
| 1 | 1 | 166 | 23.68 | 532 | 75.89 |
| 2 | 2 | 169 | 24.11 | 701 | 100.00 |

| PG3 | orig_PG3 | Frequency | Percent | Cumulative Frequency | Cumulative Percent |
|-----|----------|-----------|---------|----------------------|--------------------|
| -99 | N | 149 | 21.26 | 149 | 21.26 |
| -97 | L | 425 | 60.63 | 574 | 81.88 |
| 1 | 1 | 5 | 0.71 | 579 | 82.60 |
| 2 | 2 | 12 | 1.71 | 591 | 84.31 |
| 3 | 3 | 16 | 2.28 | 607 | 86.59 |
| 4 | 4 | 10 | 1.43 | 617 | 88.02 |
| 5 | 5 | 17 | 2.43 | 634 | 90.44 |
| 6 | 6 | 20 | 2.85 | 654 | 93.30 |
| 7 | 7 | 18 | 2.57 | 672 | 95.86 |
| 8 | 8 | 8 | 1.14 | 680 | 97.00 |
| 9 | 9 | 17 | 2.43 | 697 | 99.43 |
| 10 | 10 | 4 | 0.57 | 701 | 100.00 |

## Caution About Recoding Missing SAS Date Values

To avoid compromising your data, use only SAS missing values to indicate that the date is missing. A SAS date value is a numeric variable that can be created with the MDY function. When supplied with month, day, and year values as arguments, the MDY function returns a value that is the number of days since January 1, 1960. Program 8-2 illustrates what can happen if you assign a numeric code for missing to a SAS date variable that is missing. A DATA step creates two variables, MISSING_CODE and MISSING_DATE. MISSING_CODE contains a value that is being assigned to represent how a missing numeric variable might be coded. MISSING_DATE is the date variable that is set to equal the missing value code. PROC PRINT assigns a date FORMAT to variable MISSING_DATE to show how the values are interpreted by SAS. Listing 8-1 shows the results.

**Program 8-2: Illustrating Unexpected Results Using Numeric Missing Value Codes for SAS Date Values**

```
data date_example;
     missing_code = .;
     Study_Date = missing_code;
     output;
     missing_code = .E;
     Study_Date = missing_code;
     output;
     missing_code = -99;
     Study_Date = missing_code;
     output;
run;

proc print data=date_example;
     var missing_code Study_Date;
     format Study_Date mmddyy10.;
run;
```

Both the default SAS missing value (.) and special SAS missing value (-99) are still recognized as missing, but SAS reports the -99 value as 09/24/1959 rather than understanding it is a missing value. This would compromise any results computed with the date value because the -99 code would be treated as an actual analysis value during analysis. If you need to convert your SAS data set to a format that can be used by another analysis package other than Excel, the safest missing value to use might be default SAS missing value(.) for any SAS date variables. After your conversion, be sure to inspect the date values to make sure that the missing values were converted correctly.

**Listing 8-1: Numeric Missing Value Codes Interpreted as SAS Date Values**

| Obs | missing_code | Study_Date |
|-----|--------------|------------|
| 1   | .            | .          |
| 2   | E            | E          |
| 3   | -99          | 09/24/1959 |

# Easy Ways to Check Variable Construction

Derived variables lead the way to discovery, insights, and innovations from your project data. Not only will you be creating derived variables that are added to the data set, but data scientists and research staff will also create them for their own research investigations. Often, you will be asked to merge these derived variables with the collected data for future distribution. Your job will be to cross-check these derived variables before they are added to the data, ensuring the quality of the data set is maintained.

There are several ways to check variable construction. Programmers will often review the computer code used to create each derived variable to verify it was created correctly. There are two complications that can hamper this review:

- The computer code used to create the derived variable is not available for inspection.
- The variable was created using a computer language which the reviewer is unfamiliar and has no experience programming.

Writing a new program in SAS to re-create the derived variable, then comparing the new values with old values is another way to perform the quality control before the derived variable is added to the data set. This can be quite costly.

An easy way to check variable construction is to use SAS procedures to uncover the relationship between a derived variable and the variables used in the computation. A hidden bonus of using this technique is that you will produce a table showing your interpretation of the specifications for describing and creating the variable. Sharing this table with the person requesting or providing the derived variable will ensure that the specifications were interpreted correctly. It can also identify problems with the specifications that need to be clarified or changed before the variable has passed quality control checks and be made available to the user community.

There are two basic steps used in this method:

- Examine the relationship between the derived variables and all variables used in the computation
- Determine why the derived variable is missing

Table 8-1 shows the SAS procedures that can be used to quickly check the construction of the variable.

**Table 8-1: SAS Procedures to Examine the Relationship Between Variables**

| Type of Derived Variable | Type of Variables used in Formula for Derivation | Check with this SAS Procedure |
|---|---|---|
| Categorical | Categorical | PROC FREQ<br>PROC TABULATE |

| Type of Derived Variable | Type of Variables used in Formula for Derivation | Check with this SAS Procedure |
|---|---|---|
| Categorical | Continuous | PROC MEANS<br>PROC TABULATE |
| Continuous | Continuous | PROC REG, etc. |

The codebook for the data used in the following examples is included in Appendix C. This data set, research_data.sas7bdat, was simulated for these examples. Any similarity to actual data is a coincidence.

## Example 8-2: Checking Indicator Variables Created from Ordinal Variables

You have been asked to add several derived variables to your project's data set. These variables were created by a different programmer and are a series of indicator variables representing the categories of variable HEALTH in data set research_data.sas7bdat. Looking at the codebook in Appendix C you see that the HEALTH variable has five categories ranging from 1="Excellent" to 5="Poor." The instructions for creating these indicator variables are shown in the following list:

- If HEALTH = 1 then EXCELLENT = 1, else EXCELLENT = 0
- If HEALTH = 2 then VERYGOOD = 1, else VERYGOOD = 0
- If HEALTH = 3 then GOOD = 1, else GOOD = 0
- IF HEALTH = 4 then FAIR = 1, else FAIR = 0
- IF HEALTH = 5 then POOR = 1, else POOR = 0

From the codebook in Appendix C, you also see that some of the observations have a missing value for variable HEALTH. These specifications omit instructions on what to do if the value for variable HEALTH is missing. If you follow these instructions exactly, then when HEALTH is missing, every indicator variable would have a value of zero. The person requesting these indicator variables will want to see a table showing how the indicator variables that you created compare to the HEALTH variable. From this table, how you handle the missing category is clear to the person who requested this variable.

The programmer who created these variables followed the specifications exactly, using the SAS program shown in Program 8-3.

*Section 1:* These statements use the LIBNAME statement to assign the nickname "sas_data" to the data folder and create formats for the data.

*Section 2:* A DATA step following the exact specifications is used to create the indicator variables for the five categories of the HEALTH variable.

## Program 8-3: Creating Indicator Variables for Variable HEALTH from Exact Specifications

```
* Section 1) Assign a libref to each folder and create formats for the
data;
libname sas_data "/Data_Detective/Book/SAS_Datasets";

proc format;
    value sex 1='Male' 2='Female';
    value health 1='Excellent'
        2='Very Good'
        3='Good'
        4='Fair'
        5='Poor';
    value pass 0-59 = "Fail=0 to 59" 60-100 = "Pass=60 to 100";
    value dia_cut 60-<80 = "60 to <80" 80-89 = "80 to 89"
        90-110="90 to 110";
    value sys_cut 90-<120 = "90 to <120" 120-129 = "120 to 129"
        130-139 = "130 to 139" 140-170 = "140 to 170";
    value range30f 0-30 = "Valid Range";
    value range100f  0 - 100 = "Valid Range";
    value range300f  0 - 300 = "Valid Range";
    value take_med 0="Not on Medication" 1 = "On Medication";
run;

* Section 2) Create indicator variables for each category of the variable
HEALTH;

* Follow SPECIFICATIONS EXACTLY -- when HEALTH = . then all indicator
variables will have a value of 0. ;

data specs;
    set sas_data.research_data;

if health = 1 then  excellent = 1; else excellent = 0;
if health = 2 then verygood = 1; else verygood = 0;
if health = 3 then good = 1; else good = 0;
if health = 4 then fair = 1; else fair = 0;
if health = 5 then poor = 1; else poor = 0;

run;
```

The SAS code displaying how the indicator variables created from categories of the HEALTH variable is shown in Program 8-4.

## Program 8-4: Checking How Variable HEALTH was Created

```
proc freq data=specs;
    tables health*excellent*verygood*good*fair*poor/list missing;
    format _all_;
run;
```

## Crosstab 8-2: Indicator Variables Created from HEALTH Variable Using Exact Specifications

| health | excellent | verygood | good | fair | poor | Frequency | Percent | Cumulative Frequency | Cumulative Percent |
|---|---|---|---|---|---|---|---|---|---|
| . | 0 | 0 | 0 | 0 | 0 | 41 | 8.18 | 41 | 8.18 |
| 1 | 1 | 0 | 0 | 0 | 0 | 122 | 24.35 | 163 | 32.53 |
| 2 | 0 | 1 | 0 | 0 | 0 | 160 | 31.94 | 323 | 64.47 |
| 3 | 0 | 0 | 1 | 0 | 0 | 112 | 22.36 | 435 | 86.83 |
| 4 | 0 | 0 | 0 | 1 | 0 | 47 | 9.38 | 482 | 96.21 |
| 5 | 0 | 0 | 0 | 0 | 1 | 19 | 3.79 | 501 | 100.00 |

The crosstab shows that each indicator variable has a value of zero when HEALTH is missing. After showing this crosstab to the original programmer and the person who developed the specifications, you are asked to re-calculate the indicator variables so that all indicator variables have a value of missing when HEALTH is missing. The SAS program that you write is shown in Program 8-5 with the correct calculation for these variables. PROC FREQ is used to verify that the SAS program created each indicator variable correctly.

## Program 8-5: Correctly Handle Missing Value for Variable HEALTH

```
data health_status;
   set sas_data.research_data;

   if health=1 then
      do;
         excellent=1;
         verygood=0;
         good=0;
         fair=0;
         poor=0;
      end;
   else if health=2 then
      do;
         excellent=0;
         verygood=1;
         good=0;
         fair=0;
         poor=0;
      end;
   else if health=3 then
      do;
         excellent=0;
         verygood=0;
         good=1;
         fair=0;
         poor=0;
      end;
   else if health=4 then
      do;
         excellent=0;
         verygood=0;
```

```
              good=0;
              fair=1;
              poor=0;
          end;
      else if health=5 then
          do;
              excellent=0;
              verygood=0;
              good=0;
              fair=0;
              poor=1;
          end;
      else
          do;
              excellent=.;
              verygood=.;
              good=.;
              fair=.;
              poor=.;
          end;
  run;

  proc freq data=health_status;
      title3 'Check dummy variable creation from variable HEALTH';
      tables health*excellent*verygood*good*fair*poor/list missing;
      format _all_;
  run;
```

The table produced by PROC FREQ is shown in Crosstab 8-3. All the indicator variables now have a missing value when variable HEALTH is missing.

**Crosstab 8-3: Corrected Indicator Variables Calculated from Variable HEALTH**

| health | excellent | verygood | good | fair | poor | Frequency | Percent | Cumulative Frequency | Cumulative Percent |
|--------|-----------|----------|------|------|------|-----------|---------|----------------------|--------------------|
| . | . | . | . | . | . | 41 | 8.18 | 41 | 8.18 |
| 1 | 1 | 0 | 0 | 0 | 0 | 122 | 24.35 | 163 | 32.53 |
| 2 | 0 | 1 | 0 | 0 | 0 | 160 | 31.94 | 323 | 64.47 |
| 3 | 0 | 0 | 1 | 0 | 0 | 112 | 22.36 | 435 | 86.83 |
| 4 | 0 | 0 | 0 | 1 | 0 | 47 | 9.38 | 482 | 96.21 |
| 5 | 0 | 0 | 0 | 0 | 1 | 19 | 3.79 | 501 | 100.00 |

This example has shown how easy it is to find questionable values in derived categorical variables by creating a simple crosstab. Although you might still want to review the source code as part of your quality control checks, this crosstab is a very quick way to see a snapshot of how the programmed algorithm has handled all values of the data. This snapshot is also an effective way to show how complete the specifications are stated, as well as how they are being interpreted by the programmer.

## Example 8-3: Checking Categorical Variables Created from Continuous Variables

You have been asked to create analysis variables for the Health Club Fitness Test (HCFT). Members are tested in the following three events measuring different aspects fitness:

- Strength measured by performing push-ups: variable STRENGTH

- Endurance measured by performing sit-ups: variable ENDURANCE

- Cardiovascular fitness by completing a two-mile run: variable CARDIOVASCULAR

The scores on each of these three events range from 0 to 100. A minimum score of 60 is required to pass an event. To pass the HCFT, a member must pass all three events. You will need to create the following variables that will be included in the final data set being distributed to investigators throughout the nation:

- Number of tests taken by each member: Valid range = 0 to 3

- Pass/Fail indicator variable for each test: 0 = Fail, 1=Pass

- Number of tests passed by each member: Valid range = 0 to 3

- Total score (HCFT Score) for members who passed all three tests: 60 to 300

The codebook in Appendix C for research_data.sas7bdat shows the three variables (STRENGTH, ENDURANCE, and CARDIOVASCULAR) for the individual fitness tests. The STRENGTH and ENDURANCE variables have some missing values defined by the default SAS missing value. The CARDIOVASCULAR variable has no missing values. Program 8-3 shows SAS statements similar to the code that you would write to create and perform quality control checks on variables needed for the HCFT.

*Section 1:* These statements define the libref for the folder with the data set used in this example, a macro variable storing the name of the folder where output is written, and defines the formats used in the data set and the program.

*Section 2:* The requested variables needed for the HCFT fitness test are computed in this section. Labels are created for each variable.

*Section 3:* Quality control checks follow with PROC MEANS, PROC FREQ, and PROC REG being used to make sure the variables are created according to the specifications. Each PROC MEANS uses the missing statement to ensure missing values of the CLASS statement appears in the table produced by PROC MEANS. The TABLES statement in the PROC FREQ step uses the LIST and MISSING option. The LIST option ensures all variables will be listed in columns and the MISSING options will include the missing category in the table. Thus, all observations in the data set will be accounted for in the tables.

## Program 8-6: Checking Categorical Variables Created from Continuous Variables

```
* Section 1) Assign a libref to each folder and create formats for the
  data;
libname sas_data "/Data_Detective/Book/SAS_Datasets";
%let WorkFolder = /Data_Detective/Book/SAS_Output;

proc format;
    value sex 1='Male' 2='Female';
    value health 1='Excellent'
        2='Very Good'
        3='Good'
        4='Fair'
        5='Poor';
    value pass 0-59 = "Fail=0 to 59" 60-100 = "Pass=60 to 100";
    value dia_cut 60-<80 = "60 to <80" 80-89 = "80 to 89"
                  90-110="90 to 110";
    value sys_cut 90-<120 = "90 to <120" 120-129 = "120 to 129"
                  130-139 = "130 to 139" 140-170 = "140 to 170";
    value range30f 0-30 = "Valid Range";
    value range100f  0 - 100 = "Valid Range";
    value range300f  0 - 300 = "Valid Range";
    value take_med 0="Not on Medication" 1 = "On Medication";
    value take100f 0 - 100 = "0 - 100";
    value pass60f 0 - 59 = "Fail: 0-59" 60-100 = "Pass: 60-100";
    value pass180f 0 - 179 = "Fail 1+: 0-179"
                   180 - 300 = "Pass all 3: 180-300";
run;

* Section 2) Create variables from test scores.;
data fitness;
    set sas_data.research_data;

    Tests_taken = sum(strength>. , endurance>. , cardiovascular>.);
    label Tests_taken = "Number of fitness tests taken by each participant";

    if strength >= 60 then
        pass_strength = 1;
    else if 0<=strength<60 then
        pass_strength = 0;
    else pass_strength = .;

    if endurance >= 60 then
        pass_endurance = 1;
    else if 0<=endurance<60 then
        pass_endurance = 0;
    else pass_endurance = .;

    if cardiovascular >= 60 then
        pass_cardiovascular = 1;
    else if 0<=cardiovascular< 60 then
        pass_cardiovascular = 0;
    else pass_cardiovascular = .;
    label pass_strength = "Pass strength test (score = 60 or higher)";
    label pass_endurance = "Pass endurance test (score = 60 or higher)";
    label pass_cardiovascular = "Pass cardiovascular test (score = 60 or
higher)";
```

```
   total_passed = pass_strength + pass_endurance + pass_cardiovascular;
   label total_passed = "Number of tests passed with score of 60 or
higher";

   if total_passed = 3 then
      HCFT_score = strength + endurance + cardiovascular;
   else HCFT_score = .;
   label total_passed = "Total score for participants with scores 60 or
more on each fitness test";
run;

*Section 3) Perform Quality Control checks on the derived variables;
ods rtf file="&WorkFolder./Crosstab8_3.rtf" bodytitle;

proc freq data=fitness;
   title3 "Check TESTS_TAKEN = total number of tests taken (score
present)";
   tables tests_taken*strength*endurance*cardiovascular/list missing;
   format strength endurance cardiovascular take100f.;
run;

proc means data= fitness missing maxdec=1 n nmiss min max missing;
   title3 "Check PASS_STRENGTH (pass if score 60 or higher)";
   class pass_strength;
   var strength;
run;

proc means data= fitness missing maxdec=1 n nmiss min max missing;
   title3 "Check PASS_ENDURANCE (pass if score 60 or higher)";
   class pass_endurance;
   var endurance;
run;

proc means data= fitness missing maxdec=1 n nmiss min max missing;
   title3 "Check PASS_CARDIOVASCULAR (pass if score 60 or higher)";
   class pass_cardiovascular;
   var cardiovascular;
run;

proc freq data=fitness;
   title3 "Check TOTAL_PASSED for participants who took all 3 fitness
tests";
   tables total_passed*pass_strength*pass_endurance*pass_cardiovascular/
      list missing;
run;

proc freq data=fitness;
   title3 "Check HCFT_score=. if 1+ tests failed, has value if pass all
three tests";
   tables total_passed*HCFT_score*strength*endurance*cardiovascular/
      list missing;
   format strength endurance cardiovascular pass60f.;
   format HCFT_score pass180f.;
run;
```

```
proc reg data=fitness;
   title3 "Check HCFT_score = sum of tests if all tests passed";
   where total_passed=3;
   model HCFT_score = strength endurance cardiovascular;
run;

title3 " ";
ods rtf close;
```

The quality control check for variable TESTS_TAKEN is shown in Crosstab 8-4. PROC FREQ was used to create the table for inspecting the accuracy of the calculation for the TESTS_TAKEN variable. A format assigned to the variables STRENGTH, ENDURANCE, and CARDIOVASCULAR display the valid range of values in each cell. No out of range values occur in the data for these variables. Having a nonmissing value for these variables identifies members who completed each event and received a test score. The variable TESTS_TAKEN correctly identifies the number of members who completed each test, with 84.6% of the members having test scores in all three events.

## Crosstab 8-4: Check Variable TESTS_TAKEN = Total Number of Tests Taken (Score Present)

| Tests_taken | strength | endurance | cardiovascular | Frequency | Percent | Cumulative Frequency | Cumulative Percent |
|---|---|---|---|---|---|---|---|
| 1 | . | . | 0 - 100 | 1 | 0.20 | 1 | 0.20 |
| 2 | . | 0 - 100 | 0 - 100 | 12 | 2.40 | 13 | 2.59 |
| 2 | 0 - 100 | . | 0 - 100 | 64 | 12.77 | 77 | 15.37 |
| 3 | 0 - 100 | 0 - 100 | 0 - 100 | 424 | 84.63 | 501 | 100.00 |

PROC MEANS is used to check the derivation of indicator variables PASS_STRENGTH, PASS_ENDURANCE, PASS_CARDIOVASCULAR. Each of these variables should have a value of one if the score on the test for the relevant event was 60 or higher, a value of zero if the score was zero to 59, and a value of missing if the score was missing. The tables shown in Means 8-1 through Means 8-3 show these variables has been correctly derived.

## Means 8-1: Check Variable PASS_STRENGTH (Pass if Score 60 or Higher)

| | Analysis Variable : strength Muscular Strength (range 0 to 100 points) | | | | |
|---|---|---|---|---|---|
| pass_strength | N Obs | N | N Miss | Minimum | Maximum |
| . | 13 | 0 | 13 | . | . |
| 0 | 196 | 196 | 0 | 20.0 | 59.0 |
| 1 | 292 | 292 | 0 | 60.0 | 100.0 |

Means 8-2: Check Variable PASS_ENDURANCE (Pass if Score 60 or Higher)

| pass_endurance | N Obs | N | N Miss | Analysis Variable : endurance Endurance Test (range 0 to 100 points) Minimum | Maximum |
|---|---|---|---|---|---|
| . | 65 | 0 | 65 | . | . |
| 0 | 186 | 186 | 0 | 20.0 | 59.0 |
| 1 | 250 | 250 | 0 | 60.0 | 100.0 |

Means 8-3: Check Variable PASS_CARDIOVASCULAR (Pass if Score 60 or Higher)

| pass_cardiovascular | N Obs | N | N Miss | Analysis Variable : cardiovascular Cardiovascular Respiratory Fitness Test (range 0 to 100 points) Minimum | Maximum |
|---|---|---|---|---|---|
| 0 | 206 | 206 | 0 | 20.0 | 59.0 |
| 1 | 295 | 295 | 0 | 60.0 | 100.0 |

Variable TOTAL_PASSED is checked in Crosstab 8-5. Values of this variable are all computed as expected. TOTAL_PASSED is missing if any of the indicator variables (PASS_STRENGTH, PASS_ENDURANCE, PASS_CARDIOVASCULAR) are missing. All other values of TOTAL_PASSED are equal to sum of PASS_STRENGTH, PASS_ENDURANCE, and PASS_CARDIOVASCULAR.

Crosstab 8-5: Check Variable TOTAL_PASSED for Participants Who Took All 3 Fitness Tests

| total_passed | pass_strength | pass_endurance | pass_cardiovascular | Frequency | Percent | Cumulative Frequency | Cumulative Percent |
|---|---|---|---|---|---|---|---|
| . | . | | . | 0 | 1 | 0.20 | 1 | 0.20 |
| . | . | 1 | 0 | 5 | 1.00 | 6 | 1.20 |
| . | . | 1 | 1 | 7 | 1.40 | 13 | 2.59 |
| . | 0 | . | 0 | 7 | 1.40 | 20 | 3.99 |
| . | 0 | . | 1 | 17 | 3.39 | 37 | 7.39 |
| . | 1 | . | 0 | 20 | 3.99 | 57 | 11.38 |
| . | 1 | . | 1 | 20 | 3.99 | 77 | 15.37 |
| 0 | 0 | 0 | 0 | 35 | 6.99 | 112 | 22.36 |
| 1 | 0 | 0 | 1 | 43 | 8.58 | 155 | 30.94 |
| 1 | 0 | 1 | 0 | 34 | 6.79 | 189 | 37.72 |
| 1 | 1 | 0 | 0 | 52 | 10.38 | 241 | 48.10 |
| 2 | 0 | 1 | 1 | 60 | 11.98 | 301 | 60.08 |
| 2 | 1 | 0 | 1 | 56 | 11.18 | 357 | 71.26 |
| 2 | 1 | 1 | 0 | 52 | 10.38 | 409 | 81.64 |
| 3 | 1 | 1 | 1 | 92 | 18.36 | 501 | 100.00 |

HCFT_score is checked in Crosstab 8-6. This crosstab can be used to check both TOTAL_PASSED and HCFT_Score. A format is used to group the STRENGTH, ENDURANCE, and CARDIOVASCULAR event scores into "Pass" and "Fail" categories using a cutpoint of 60. TOTAL_PASSED correctly counts the test scores in rows that have scores for all three tests and has a missing score if any of the three event scores are missing. HCFT_SCORE only has a nonmissing value if all three event scores are in the "Pass"category.

**Crosstab 8-6: Check HCFT_SCORE=. if 1+ Tests Failed, Has Value if a Member Passes All Three Tests**

| total_passed | HCFT_score | strength | endurance | cardiovascular | Frequency | Percent | Cumulative Frequency | Cumulative Percent |
|---|---|---|---|---|---|---|---|---|
| . | . | . | . | Fail: 0-59 | 1 | 0.20 | 1 | 0.20 |
| . | . | . | Pass: 60-100 | Fail: 0-59 | 5 | 1.00 | 6 | 1.20 |
| . | . | . | Pass: 60-100 | Pass: 60-100 | 7 | 1.40 | 13 | 2.59 |
| . | . | Fail: 0-59 | . | Fail: 0-59 | 7 | 1.40 | 20 | 3.99 |
| . | . | Fail: 0-59 | . | Pass: 60-100 | 17 | 3.39 | 37 | 7.39 |
| . | . | Pass: 60-100 | . | Fail: 0-59 | 20 | 3.99 | 57 | 11.38 |
| . | . | Pass: 60-100 | . | Pass: 60-100 | 20 | 3.99 | 77 | 15.37 |
| 0 | . | Fail: 0-59 | Fail: 0-59 | Fail: 0-59 | 35 | 6.99 | 112 | 22.36 |
| 1 | . | Fail: 0-59 | Fail: 0-59 | Pass: 60-100 | 43 | 8.58 | 155 | 30.94 |
| 1 | . | Fail: 0-59 | Pass: 60-100 | Fail: 0-59 | 34 | 6.79 | 189 | 37.72 |
| 1 | . | Pass: 60-100 | Fail: 0-59 | Fail: 0-59 | 52 | 10.38 | 241 | 48.10 |
| 2 | . | Fail: 0-59 | Pass: 60-100 | Pass: 60-100 | 60 | 11.98 | 301 | 60.08 |
| 2 | . | Pass: 60-100 | Fail: 0-59 | Pass: 60-100 | 56 | 11.18 | 357 | 71.26 |
| 2 | . | Pass: 60-100 | Pass: 60-100 | Fail: 0-59 | 52 | 10.38 | 409 | 81.64 |
| 3 | Pass all 3: 180-300 | Pass: 60-100 | Pass: 60-100 | Pass: 60-100 | 92 | 18.36 | 501 | 100.00 |

A quick way to check that HCFT_score is the sum of the three test scores for members who passed each test with a score of 60 points or higher is to use regression to see whether the following model fits perfectly:

$$HCFT\_score = b_0 + b_1*STRENGTH + b_2*ENDURANCE + b_3*CARDIOVASCULAR$$

## Regression 8-1: Check HCFT_SCORE = Sum of Tests if All Tests Passed

*The REG Procedure*
*Model: MODEL1*
*Dependent Variable: HCFT_score*

| Number of Observations Read | 92 |
|---|---|
| Number of Observations Used | 92 |

| Analysis of Variance | | | | | |
|---|---|---|---|---|---|
| Source | DF | Sum of Squares | Mean Square | F Value | Pr > F |
| Model | 3 | 58399 | 19466 | Infty | <.0001 | ←Infty means a perfect fit
| Error | 88 | 0 | 0 | | |
| Corrected Total | 91 | 58399 | | | |

| Root MSE | 0 | R-Square | 1.0000 |
|---|---|---|---|
| Dependent Mean | 261.85870 | Adj R-Sq | 1.0000 |
| Coeff Var | 0 | | |

| Parameter Estimates | | | | | | |
|---|---|---|---|---|---|---|
| Variable | Label | DF | Parameter Estimate | Standard Error | t Value | Pr > \|t\| |
| Intercept | Intercept | 1 | -4.1638E-12 | 0 | -Infty | <.0001 |
| strength | Muscular Strength (range 0 to 100 points) | 1 | 1.00000 | 0 | Infty | <.0001 |
| endurance | Endurance Test (range 0 to 100 points) | 1 | 1.00000 | 0 | Infty | <.0001 |
| cardiovascular | Cardiovascular Respiratory Fitness Test (range 0 to 100 points) | 1 | 1.00000 | 0 | Infty | <.0001 |

↑
Parameter
Estimates =
Coefficients in
Model

↑
Infty means a
perfect fit

A perfect fit would estimate the intercept $b_0 = 0$ and the other parameter estimates would be $b_1 = 1$, $b_2 = 1$, and $b_3 = 1$. The Model F-Value would be infinity as would the value of the t-statistics in the Parameter Estimate table. This is what we see in the estimates from the results displayed in Regression 8-1. The estimate of the intercept, $-4.1638*10^{-12}$, is expressed in scientific notation and is equivalent to 0 given the rounding error from the model fitting process.

## Summary

This chapter has covered two important tasks in the final stages of preparing data for analysis and distribution. The first task is to add codes to variables to identify why a variable is missing. This provides essential information used in analysis to clearly comprehend why data is missing. Different reasons that can influence how a user interprets missing values during analysis are listed below:

- Missing because participant did not answer a question
- Missing because question was not part of survey at time of interview
- Missing because legitimately skipped over as part of skip pattern

The second task is extending quality control methods to validate variables derived from other variables in the data set. Often these derived variables are included as part of the final data set. This chapter presented very cost-effective ways to extend quality control to the derived variables by using SAS procedures to discover the relationship between the derived variable and the variables used in the derivation. With just a few lines of code to run PROC FREQ, PROC MEANS, or PROC REG, you can uncover the details of design and construction of many derived variables by examining the output from these procedures. If inconsistencies are uncovered, this aids designing SAS code to create an improved version of the derived variable.

If you have followed the recommendations in this book, your data will be of high quality and ready for research and publication. Your work has been instrumental in moving your project data from Stage 4 (Preparation) to Stage 6 (Publish Results) in the data life cycle described in Appendix A. Stage 7 through Stage 9 in Appendix A describe activities to wrap up your project. These stages include the following:

- Stage 7: Preserving versions of your project data used in publications
- Stage 8: Preparing data for sharing with outside users
- Stage 9: Final archive of data

Your data is priceless. Appendix A provides a checklist of activities for every stage in the data life cycle to produce robust and high quality data. Review the checklists for Stage 4 through Stage 6 and you will see how the techniques and SAS macro programs that you learned to use support these data preparation tasks. Your work has given your data a long and usable life. The checklists for Stage 7 through Stage 9 will guide you in archiving published analyses and project data. This ensures that your data is always usable and ready to be restored for new research activities.

# Appendix A: Your Part in the Data Life Cycle

## Introduction

This appendix explains the data life cycle, describing how quality control and good documentation help the data flow through each stage. You will discover how using techniques from the *Data Detective's Toolkit* throughout the data life cycle lowers the costs of data preparation, automates documentation, improves data quality, and extends the lifetime of your data.

## Understanding the Data Life Cycle

The data life cycle is the series of stages your data flows through from conception to archive. Figure A-1 shows the stages in the data life cycle embedded in the context of critical tasks performed continually across all stages. Activities in each stage produce one or more project assets (data sets or documents) used in subsequent stages. Performing the critical tasks of documenting, safeguarding, and managing quality continually throughout the data life cycle will ensure that all data produced in your project is ready for research and easy to use.

Managers, research investigators, and programmers work together at every step throughout the life cycle. The following teams perform critical roles in advancing this process:

- The management Team comprised of the managers, research investigators, and policy makers who are responsible for project conception and will act on the insights uncovered by the analytics team

- The programming Team responsible for collecting or obtaining existing data, data cleaning, restructuring, and the aggregation of acquired data when needed

- The analytics Team focuses on analyzing the data to assess quality, create study-wide variables, and find meaningful insights

For many projects, a team might have only one member responsible for critical tasks or might have members working in different capacities across multiple teams.

**Figure A-1: Stages in the Data Life Cycle**

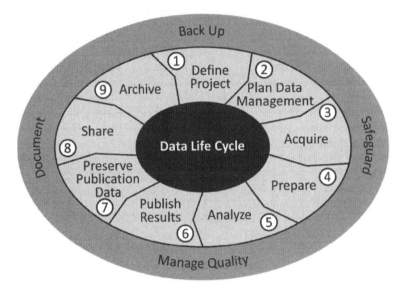

You will use the techniques and data tools described in this book from Stage 4 through Stage 9. The following descriptions of the data life cycle provide details of the activities your team will work on in each stage. Although Stage 1 and Stage 2 do not use the *Data Detective's Toolkit*, details are included here to provide a better context for understanding how and where your role as a programmer fits into the big picture.

## Stage 1: Define Project

The primary goal of this stage is to create a concise description of the purpose, use, and products that need to be delivered at the end of the project. This proposal is overseen by the management team working to establish what the sponsor or lead research investigators need and what the project is expected to accomplish. The following items are identified in the project proposal:

- A clear statement of the reason for the project that functions as a high-level analysis plan. This includes a description of the scientific aims or problem being investigated, purpose of the project, scope of the investigation, and the methods and design that will be used to acquire and analyze the data

- Sources of data identified (new data, existing data, or a combination of both)

- A description of products or project assets that need to be delivered at the end of the project, including data files, documentation, social media products, reports, and publications

- A list of potential users of the project assets

- Resources needed to collect and process the data, including funding and personnel

- Archive requirements

- Data sharing policy

- Data security requirements

- Distribution requirements

## Stage 2: Plan Data Management

The data management plan is created by representatives from the programming and analytics teams. It establishes how the data will be handled during the project as well as after the project has ended. It describes the criteria for how each project asset will be obtained or produced. The plan should define the strategy for handling data in each of the remaining stages of the life cycle. This plan includes the following tasks:

- Method of acquiring data

- Requirements for processing and cleaning data

- Production of response rates and bias estimates

- Data analysis requirements

- Safeguarding of data and other assets during the project

- Publications created from the project assets

- Data Sharing requirements

- Archive plan

The description of each of these tasks will also include requirements for quality assurance and documentation. The hours that it takes to complete the data management plan can save weeks of programming and troubleshooting at each stage. A carefully articulated plan helps to keep your project within budget and on schedule.

## Stage 3: Acquire Data

Data acquired during this stage can be an original collection of new data, existing data obtained from various sources, or a combination of both. This is the stage where the *Data Detective's Toolkit* will start being useful, especially in the Extract and Document activities. Your programming team undertakes many different activities in this stage such as:

- Review and test data collection questionnaires, instrumentation, and methods before being deployed
- Design new systems to collect data
- Establish infrastructure for storing the data
- Extract data from multiple sources
- Verify structure of data sets (number of variables, number of observations, unique record identifiers, linkage between data sets)
- Evaluate and obtain existing data sets for reuse
- Document the source of the data, the structure of the data, and any anomalies occurring during acquisition
- Incorporate feedback and address issues discovered by programmers in the Preparation or Analysis stage

Data can be very diverse in nature, such as a survey of individuals, production data, meteorological data, biological data, excerpts from social media sources. Members of the programming team will create one or more raw data sets used in the next stage of preparing the data.

## Stage 4: Prepare Data

The data preparation stage is where using the *Data Detective's Toolkit* really contributes to establishing quality control monitoring. Unexpected or missing values, conflicting information, incorrect flow through skip patterns, incomplete data, combining multiple data sets with different attributes, attrition of participants, and changes in data collection methods or instruments during collection requires careful investigation and alleviation during preparation.

In this stage, programmers transform raw data sets into research-friendly data sets by performing the following activities:

- Download data sets from the data collection systems or repositories
- Combine data sets with different formats and structures
- Create SAS labels and formats for each variable in the raw data sets and, if necessary, data sets obtained from outside sources
- Run quality control checks on each variable from all the data sets including range of values, skip pattern validation, and comparison of estimates from collected data to estimates from outside sources

- Edit data when appropriate to correct anomalies uncovered during the quality control checks

- Create new variables based on or calculated from existing variables

- Incorporate feedback and address issues reported by the analytics teams activities in the analysis stage

- Create documentation for data sets including codebooks, users' manuals, data catalogs, and crosswalks

By performing these activities, your programming team provides the analysis team with easy to use, well-documented data sets ready for investigation.

## Stage 5: Analyze Data

Your analytics team will use the data sets from the previous stage to assess data quality as well as investigate statistical hypotheses together with sponsors and lead research investigators.

If documentation and quality control activities are built into the system at the beginning of data collection or acquisition, analysts can examine the data early in the project on a flow basis. Quality control ensures the data sets contain available information to provide evidence whether a belief or scientific hypothesis is true or valid. Documentation provides the instructions to correctly use and analyze the data. Your analytics team will make immediate use of the preliminary codebooks, users' manuals, data catalogs, and crosswalks created during data preparation. These documents provide information to determine what is in the data set, what each data item means, and how the data sets are related.

During this stage, your analytics team contributes to the project with programming activities to create the final, cleaned data:

- For Population Surveys,

  - If needed, compute sampling weights to adjust for oversampling of select populations during analysis

  - Assess quality by calculating response rates and performing bias analysis to determine how well your data matches the target population

- Identify anomalies in the data that were not reconciled in the preparation stage

- Work with the programming team to investigate any discrepancies and suspicious results

- Prepare reports, manuscripts, and articles for publication or distribution through websites or social media

Comments and recommendations from the analytics team can be sent back to the preparation stage to improve the quality of the data and be incorporated into the codebooks, users' manuals, data catalogs, and crosswalks.

## Stage 6: Publish Results

This stage ensures the reports, publications, and other results created by the analytics team are available for general review. Your analytics team should ensure they can replicate any analysis results used in the publications by taking these steps:

- Review all programs used to create new variables for analysis or execute analysis, include comments and instructions for running programs
- Re-run the programs to create new variables and validate construction of new variables
- Re-run the analysis for the results used in your manuscript, compare outputs from programs to tables and figures in the manuscript

You can now be confident that the results from your analysis can be replicated and are ready for publication. The distribution of the findings might be a formal report to the funding agency or select individuals in a company or there might be a wider distribution through peer-reviewed journals, websites, social media, news releases, and other venues.

## Stage 7: Preserve Publication Data

The preservation stage ensures that programs and data used in any scheduled release of data or manuscripts accepted for publication are stored for safety and retrieval when needed. This should be done in conjunction with all publications from your analytics team but extends to anyone who publishes results from the data. This storage is in addition to the regularly scheduled backup of project activities or final archive of project data. While the activities in this stage are very similar to those in Stage 9 when you are creating the final archive, the purpose here is to ensure that snapshots of the data are saved at strategic time points during the lifetime of the data.

What data should be included? Data needed to validate research findings in publications or information released to the general public. This includes data that are published in theses, dissertations, refereed journal articles, supplemental data attachments for manuscripts, books, and book chapters, and other print or electronic publication formats. The following list of items need to be saved to preserve the publication and steps to create it:

- Final data sets and documentation
- Analyzed data sets
- SAS Programs
- SAS Output
- SAS log files
- Copy of publication

Since the quality of data can be continually improved during the life cycle, it is important to preserve the version of the data set used during analysis along with the final publication of analytic findings. These data sets should include internal, constructed, interim, or intermediate variables that were constructed during analysis and are accessible to replicate results or further explore results released in the next stage.

## Stage 8: Share Data

Many projects include sharing the final data with outside users. At this stage, your team should have final data, codebooks, crosswalks, and user manuals available. Funding agencies might require research products such as data and associated documentation to be available to the general public. Other agencies might restrict the users who are granted use of the data. Some data sets might have restrictions based on data security or Institutional Review Board (IRB) requirements.

The data prepared for sharing might differ from the final data in many respects. Certain variables might be deleted from the final data sets when creating the shared data. Usually, all variables that can be used to identify an individual or other protected entity are removed from the shared data. A data set designed for sharing might also have values of variables aggregated over groups of observations rather than values from the original individual observations. This is done to prevent deductive disclosure of the individual or entity contributing data to the project.

Your team uses the data management plan and data security plan to create a data sharing strategy that includes the following:

- What data can be shared?
- Who can use the data?
- Will a formal data use agreement be required?
- When will the data be available?
- Where will the shared data be located?
- What data documentation is necessary to use the data?
- How does someone get the data?
- How long can someone use the data?

## Stage 9: Archive Project

The primary goal of this stage is the safe storage of programs, initial raw data, final data, and final documentation to ensure future accessibility of the data. This step has many activities that are identical to Stage 7. The main purpose of this step is to archive the data at the end of its life. This ensures that it can be resurrected anytime it is needed.

To ensure the data can be used in the future, your team will save both data and documentation in formats that can be read or converted to many different platforms. Your documentation accompanying the data sets should include enough supporting information to understand the content and structure of the data files, how the files are related to each other, and how they were created.

Your team will review all data and documentation to identify confidentiality risks and take steps to minimize risk. Care should also be taken to remove any data records or variables that are authorized to be removed from that data at end of project. This should also include removing variables that are personal identifiers or protected health information.

The following checklist helps in preparing your data sets and documentation for archiving:

- Data sets
  - Initial raw data sets
  - Final cleaned data sets (include variable labels and formats)
- Data sets stored in one or more common file formats suitable for long-term preservation
  - SAS
  - SPSS
  - Stata
  - R
  - Excel
  - Comma-separated values (.csv)
- All SAS programs used for preparing data and documentation
- Data documentation
  - Codebooks
  - Crosswalks
  - Data catalogs
  - Data collection instruments and protocol
  - Lab protocol and instrument descriptions
  - Methodology reports
  - Users guides
  - README files
- Documentation format
  - Text
  - Microsoft Word
  - Adobe portable document format (.pdf)

Data from your project is now ready to be archived. With good documentation your data set has the potential to be restored for additional use and research activities.

## Summary

This appendix provides an overview of the stages involved in the successful preparation, management, and preservation of your project data for use and reuse. Each project is unique, and this description of the data life cycle can easily be adapted to meet the needs of your project. The description of each stage of the data life cycle includes a list of activities and products providing a useful checklist for project staff.

The *Data Detective's Toolkit* can be used to automate cleaning, preparing, and managing your data from Stage 3 (Acquire Data) all the way to Stage 9 (Archive Project). Use of the macro toolkit reduces your workload and improves overall quality of the final data. Perhaps the most important point for you to note is the following: *If you want to stay on time and within budget, implement data preparation activities at the beginning of data acquisition, so you are always producing the clean, research-friendly data set you need at the end of the project.* The macro programs provided with the *Data Detective's Toolkit* are designed to enable you to do this with minimal effort.

# Appendix B: Skip Pattern Data Codebook

## Introduction

This appendix contains the SAS program used to create a codebook for the "Skip Pattern" data set used in the Chapter 7 examples. This is the cleaned version of the data after all skip patterns in the raw data have been audited and corrected. This raw skip pattern data was simulated for the examples. Any similarity to actual data is merely a coincidence.

## SAS Program to Create Codebook

Program B-1 shows the SAS statements to create the codebook shown in Codebook B-1.

*Section 1:* In-line formatting is used in the TITLE and FOOTNOTE statements to customize the justification, font, and font size used in the codebook.

*Section 2:* Macro variables are used to store the location of folders for the *Data Detective's Toolkit* SAS programs, the data set that will be used to create the codebook, and the folder where the output will be saved.

*Section 3:* PROC FORMAT is used to create the formats assigned to variables in the data set. Note that the special SAS missing values of .L and .N are included in the VALUE statements for many of the formats.

*Section 4:* The %TK_codebook macro is invoked to create the codebook. The parameters are used to identify:

- The libref where the data set is stored (lib=work)
- The name of the SAS data set (file1=skippatterndata_cln)
- The libref where the format library is stored (fmtlib=work)
- The ODS destination for the type of codebook you want to create (cb_type=RTF)

- The name of the file that you want to store the codebook (cb_file = &cb_name).

  ○ &cb_name is the macro variable that was created in Section 2 to hold the name of the codebook that you want to create.

- The order you want the variables listed in the codebook (var_order=internal)

  ○ The internal keyword tells %TK_codebook that you want the variables listed in the same order as they are stored in the SAS data set.

- The size of the codebook (cb_size=FULL) indicates you want all information listed on every variable.

- The organization of the codebook (organization=One record per Participant (CASEID), which will be included with the data set information at the beginning of the codebook.

- The flag for the potential problem reports (include_warn=NO), which is turned off. These reports were examined when the data set was created, with all problems investigated and solved.

## Program B-1: Create Codebook for the Skip Pattern Data Set Created in Chapter 7

```
* Section 1) Add options to embellish titles and footnotes;
title j=center height=10pt font=Arial Bold Italic "Cleaned Skip Pattern
Data Codebook from Chapter 7";
footnote j=left height=9pt font=Arial "Data created for illustrating the
Data Detective's Toolkit.";

* Section 2) Define folders, name of codebook, and include codebook
  program;
%let TKFolder = /Data_Detective/Book/SAS_programs/TK_toolkit;
%let DataFolder = /Data_Detective/Book/SAS_Datasets;
%let WorkFolder = /Data_Detective/Book/SAS_Output;
libname SAS_data "&DataFolder";
%let cb_name=&WorkFolder/CodebookB_1.rtf;

%include "&TKFolder/TK_codebook.sas";

* Section 3) Create formats;
proc format;
    value VERSION 1='Pilot' 2='Production';
    value DEM1f 18 - 99 = "Valid Range";
    value DEM2f 1-'Female' 2='Male';
    value DEM3f 1 = 'White'
        2 = 'Black or African American'
        3 = 'Hispanic'
        4 = 'Asian'
        5 = 'Other'
        6 = 'Refused';
    value DEM4f 1 = "< High School"
        2 = 'High School Graduate/GED'
        3 = "Some College/vocational school (no degree)"
        4 = "2-year college/vocational/Associate's degree"
        5 = "4-year college or higher (BA, BS, MA, MS, PhD)"
    ;
    value TOB1f 1 = "Yes" 2 = "No (Go to Section 3)";
    value TOB2f 0-30= "Valid Range"   .L = "Legitimate Skip"
        .E="Expected Reply, Not Answered";
```

```
      value TOB3f 1 = "Yes" 2 = "No "  .L = "Legitimate Skip"
         .E="Expected Reply, Not Answered";
      value TOB4f 1 = "Yes" 2 = "No "  .L = "Legitimate Skip"
         .E="Expected Reply, Not Answered";
      value TOB5f 1 = "Smoke the same amount"
         2 = "Increase the amount of cigarettes smoked"
         3 = "Decrease the amount of cigarettes smoked"
         4 = "Quit smoking cigarettes altogether"
         .L = "Legitimate Skip"
         .E="Expected Reply, Not Answered";
      value PG1f 1 = "Yes" 2 = "No (Go to End of Survey)"
         .L = "Legitimate Skip" .E="Expected Reply, Not Answered";
      value PG2f 1 - 10 ="Valid Range" .L = "Legitimate Skip"
         .E="Expected Reply, Not Answered";
      value PG3f 1 - 10 ="Valid Range" .L = "Legitimate Skip"
         .N = "Question Not Available" .E="Expected Reply, Not Answered";
      value PG4f 1 = "Yes" 2 = "No (Go to End of Survey)"
         3 = "Unsure (Go to End of Survey)" .L = "Legitimate Skip"
         .E="Expected Reply, Not Answered";
      value PG5f 0 - 9 ="Valid Range"  .L = "Legitimate Skip"
         .E="Expected Reply, Not Answered";
      value $anytext ' '='Missing (blank)' other='Text or value supplied';
      value $showall default = 20 ' '='Missing (blank)';
      value shownum . = 'SAS Missing (.)' other = _same_;
      value anymiss .='SAS Missing (.)' other='Any Number';
      value version 1 = "Date started: June 15, 2020"
         2 = "Date started: July 31, 2020";
      value MODE 1 = "WEB" 2 = "MAIL";
   run;

   data work.skippatterndata_cln(label="Cleaned Skip Pattern Data");
      set SAS_data.skippatterndata_cln;
      format svy_mode mode.;
      format version version.;
   run;

   * Section 4) Create codebook;
   %TK_codebook(lib=work,
      file1=skippatterndata_cln,
      fmtlib=work,
      cb_type=RTF,
      cb_file=&cb_name,
      var_order=internal,
      cb_size=BRIEF,
      organization = One record per Participant (CASEID),
      include_warn=NO);
   run;
```

The codebook is shown in Codebook B-1.

## Codebook B-1: Codebook for the Cleaned Skip Pattern Data Set from Chapter 7
### *Cleaned Skip Pattern Data Codebook from Chapter 7*

*Data Set: skippatterndata_cln.sas7bdat*
*Label: Cleaned Skip Pattern Data*
*Date Created: 17NOV20:21:58:16*
*Number of Observations: 701     Number of Variables: 17*
*Organization of Data Set: One record per Participant (CASEID)*

| Variable Name | Label | Type | Values | Frequency Category | Frequency | Percent |
|---|---|---|---|---|---|---|
| CASEID | Unique identifier for participant | Num 8 | . | SAS missing (.) | 0 | 0.00 |
| | | | 10000 to 10700 | Range | 701 | 100.00 |
| SVY_MODE | MODE of Data Collection (1=WEB, 2=MAIL) | Num 8 | 1 | WEB | 348 | 49.64 |
| | | | 2 | MAIL | 353 | 50.36 |
| VERSION | VERSION of Data Collection Instrument: 1=Pilot, 2=Production | Num 8 | 1 | Date started: June 15, 2020 | 149 | 21.26 |
| | | | 2 | Date started: July 31, 2020 | 552 | 78.74 |
| DEM1 | How old are you? | Num 8 | . | SAS missing (.) | 61 | 8.70 |
| | | | 18-99 | Valid Range | 640 | 91.30 |
| DEM2 | Sex of participant | Num 8 | 1 | Female | 331 | 47.22 |
| | | | 2 | Male | 370 | 52.78 |
| DEM3 | Race/Ethnicity | Num 8 | . | SAS missing (.) | 24 | 3.42 |
| | | | 1 | White | 408 | 58.20 |
| | | | 2 | Black or African American | 162 | 23.11 |
| | | | 3 | Hispanic | 58 | 8.27 |
| | | | 4 | Asian | 20 | 2.85 |
| | | | 5 | Other | 17 | 2.43 |
| | | | 6 | Refused | 12 | 1.71 |
| DEM4 | Highest grade/year of school completed | Num 8 | 1 | < High School | 46 | 6.56 |
| | | | 2 | High School Graduate/GED | 137 | 19.54 |
| | | | 3 | Some College/vocational school (no degree) | 179 | 25.53 |

| | | | | | | |
|---|---|---|---|---|---|---|
| | | | 4 | 2-year college/vocational/Associate's degree | 114 | 16.26 |
| | | | 5 | 4-year college or higher (BA, BS, MA, MS, PhD) | 225 | 32.10 |
| TOB1 | Ever smoked a cigarette, even one or two puffs? | Num 8 | 1 | Yes | 342 | 48.79 |
| | | | 2 | No (Go to Section 3) | 359 | 51.21 |
| TOB2 | [Ask if TOB1=1] On how many of the past 30 days did you smoke a cigarette? | Num 8 | .L | Legitimate Skip | 359 | 51.21 |
| | | | 0-30 | Valid Range | 342 | 48.79 |
| TOB3 | [Ask if TOB1=1] Smoked at least 100 cigarettes in your life? | Num 8 | .E | Expected Reply, Not Answered | 7 | 1.00 |
| | | | .L | Legitimate Skip | 359 | 51.21 |
| | | | 1 | Yes | 166 | 23.68 |
| | | | 2 | No | 169 | 24.11 |
| TOB4 | [Ask if TOB1=1] Stopped smoking cigarettes for 1 or more days because trying to quit? | Num 8 | .L | Legitimate Skip | 359 | 51.21 |
| | | | 1 | Yes | 190 | 27.10 |
| | | | 2 | No | 152 | 21.68 |
| TOB5 | [Ask if TOB1=1 and TOB2>0] In the next 3 months do you think your will ... | Num 8 | .E | Expected Reply, Not Answered | 39 | 5.56 |
| | | | .L | Legitimate Skip | 365 | 52.07 |
| | | | 1 | Smoke the same amount | 175 | 24.96 |
| | | | 2 | Increase the amount of cigarettes smoked | 75 | 10.70 |
| | | | 3 | Decrease the amount of cigarettes smoked | 23 | 3.28 |
| | | | 4 | Quit smoking cigarettes altogether | 24 | 3.42 |

| | | | | | | |
|---|---|---|---|---|---|---|
| PG1 | [Ask if DEM2=1] Ever been pregnant? | Num 8 | .L | Legitimate Skip | 370 | 52.78 |
| | | | 1 | Yes | 159 | 22.68 |
| | | | 2 | No (Go to End of Survey) | 172 | 24.54 |
| PG2 | [Ask if DEM2=1 AND PG1=1] How many pregnancies have you had? | Num 8 | .L | Legitimate Skip | 542 | 77.32 |
| | | | 1-10 | Valid Range | 159 | 22.68 |
| PG3 | [Ask if DEM2=1 AND PG1=1 AND VERSION>1] How many pregnancies did you have that did not result in live birth? | Num 8 | .L | Legitimate Skip | 425 | 60.63 |
| | | | .N | Question Not Available | 149 | 21.26 |
| | | | 1-10 | Valid Range | 127 | 18.12 |
| PG4 | [Ask if DEM2=1 AND PG1=1] Are you pregnant now? | Num 8 | .L | Legitimate Skip | 542 | 77.32 |
| | | | 1 | Yes | 41 | 5.85 |
| | | | 2 | No (Go to End of Survey) | 79 | 11.27 |
| | | | 3 | Unsure (Go to End of Survey) | 39 | 5.56 |
| PG5 | [Ask if DEM2=1 AND PG4=1 AND PG1=1] How many months pregnant are you? | Num 8 | .L | Legitimate Skip | 660 | 94.15 |
| | | | 0-9 | Valid Range | 41 | 5.85 |

# Appendix C: Research Data Codebook

## Introduction

This appendix contains the SAS program and output used to create the codebook for the "Research" data set used in Chapter 8 examples. This data was simulated for the examples. Any similarity to actual data is purely a coincidence.

## SAS Program to Create Codebook

Program C-1 shows the SAS statements to create the codebook shown in Codebook C-1.

*Section 1:* This section uses in-line formatting to customize the justification, font, and font size for the title and footnote used on the codebook.

*Section 2:* Macro variables are used to store the location of folders for the *Data Detective's Toolkit* SAS programs, the data set that will be used to create the codebook, and the folder where the output will be saved.

*Section 3:* This section contains the PROC FORMAT statements used to create the formats assigned to variables in the data set.

*Section 4:* The %TK_codebook macro is invoked to create the codebook. The parameters are used to identify:

- The libref where the data set is stored (lib=SAS_data)

- The name of the SAS data set (file1=Research_data)

- The libref where the format library is stored (fmtlib=work)

- The ODS destination for the type of codebook you want to create (cb_type=RTF)

- The name of the file that you want to store the codebook (cb_file = &cb_name).

    - &cb_name is the macro variable that was created to hold the name of the codebook that you want to create.

- The order you want the variables listed in the codebook (var_order=internal)

    ○ The internal keyword tells %TK_codebook that you want the variables listed in the same order as they are stored in the SAS data set.

- The size of the codebook (cb_size=BRIEF) indicates you want condensed information listed on every variable.

- The organization of the codebook (organization=One record per Participant (CASEID) ), which will be included with the data set information at the beginning of the codebook.

- The flag for the potential problem reports (include_warn=NO), which is turned off. These reports were examined when the data set was created, with all problems investigated and solved.

## Program C-1: Codebook for Data Set Used in Chapter 8 Examples

```
* Section 1) Add options to embellish titles and footnotes;
title j=center height=10pt font=Arial Bold Italic  bcolor="LTGRAY"
"Research Data Codebook for Chapter 8 Examples";
footnote j=left height=9pt font=Arial "Data created for illustrating the
Data Detective's Toolkit.";


* Section 2) Define folders, name of codebook, and include codebook
program;
%let TKFolder = /Data_Detective/Book/SAS_programs/TK_toolkit;
%let DataFolder = /Data_Detective/Book/SAS_Datasets;
%let WorkFolder = /Data_Detective/Book/SAS_Output;
libname SAS_data "&DataFolder";
%let cb_name=&WorkFolder/CodebookC_1.rtf;


%include "&TKFolder/TK_codebook.sas";


* Section 3) Formats for variables in data set;
proc format;
    value sex 1='Male' 2='Female';
    value health 1='Excellent'
        2='Very Good'
        3='Good'
        4='Fair'
        5='Poor';
    value pass 0-59 = "Fail=0 to 59" 60-100 = "Pass=60 to 100";
    value dia_cut 60-<80 = "60 to <80" 80-89 = "80 to 89" 90-110="90 to
110";
    value sys_cut 90-<120 = "90 to <120" 120-129 = "120 to 129" 130-139 =
"130 to 139" 140-170 = "140 to 170";
    value range30f 0-30 = "Valid Range";
    value range100f  0-100 = "Valid Range";
    value range300f  0-300 = "Valid Range";
    value take_med 0="Not on Medication" 1 = "On Medication";
    value age 25-50 = "Valid Range";
    value systolic 90-170 = "Valid Range (units=mm Hg)";
    value diastolic 60-110 = "Valid Range (units=mm Hg)";
run;


* Section 4) Create codebook;
%TK_codebook(lib=SAS_data,
    file1=Research_data,
```

```
    fmtlib=work,
    cb_type=RTF,
    cb_file=&cb_name,
    var_order=internal,
    cb_size=BRIEF,
    organization = One record per Participant (CASEID),
    include_warn=NO);
run;
```

The codebook appears in Codebook C-1.

## Codebook C-1: Codebook for the Research Data Set Used in Chapter 8

### *Research Data Codebook for Chapter 8 Examples*

*Data Set: Research_data.sas7bdat*
*Label: Simulated Data for Examples*
*Date Created: 28AUG20:13:56:13*
*Number of Observations: 501    Number of Variables: 14*
*Organization of Data Set: One record per Participant (CASEID)*

| Variable Name | Label | Type | Values | Frequency Category | Frequency | Percent |
|---|---|---|---|---|---|---|
| CASEID | Unique Identifier for Participant | Num 8 | | SAS missing (.) | 0 | 0.00 |
| | | | 10000 to 10500 | Range | 501 | 100.00 |
| INT_DATE | Interview date | Num 8 | | SAS missing (.) | 0 | 0.00 |
| | | | 03/21/2017 to 04/20/2017 | Range | 501 | 100.00 |
| BIRTHDATE | Date of Birth | Num 8 | | SAS missing (.) | 40 | 7.98 |
| | | | 05/25/1967 to 02/12/1992 | Range | 461 | 92.02 |
| AGE | Age at time of interview | Num 8 | | Missing (blank) | 40 | 7.98 |
| | | | 25-50 | Valid Range | 461 | 92.02 |
| SEX | Sex of participant | Num 8 | 1 | Male | 247 | 49.30 |
| | | | 2 | Female | 254 | 50.70 |

| Name | Description | Type | Value/Range | Label | Count | % |
|---|---|---|---|---|---|---|
| EXER_DAYS | In the Past 30 days, how many days did you exercise at least 60 minutes? | Num 8 | 0-30 | Valid Range | 501 | 100.00 |
| HEALTH | How is your health? | Num 8 | | Missing (blank) | 41 | 8.18 |
| | | | 1 | Excellent | 122 | 24.35 |
| | | | 2 | Very Good | 160 | 31.94 |
| | | | 3 | Good | 112 | 22.36 |
| | | | 4 | Fair | 47 | 9.38 |
| | | | 5 | Poor | 19 | 3.79 |
| STRENGTH | Muscular Strength (range 0 to 100 points) | Num 8 | | Missing (blank) | 13 | 2.59 |
| | | | 0-100 | Valid Range | 488 | 97.41 |
| ENDURANCE | Endurance Test (range 0 to 100 points) | Num 8 | | Missing (blank) | 65 | 12.97 |
| | | | 0-100 | Valid Range | 436 | 87.03 |
| CARDIOVASCULAR | Cardiovascular Respiratory Fitness Test (range 0 to 100 points) | Num 8 | 0-100 | Valid Range | 501 | 100.00 |
| TOTAL_FITNESS | Total Fitness score = STRENGTH + ENDURANCE + CARDIOVASCULAR | Num 8 | | Missing (blank) | 77 | 15.37 |
| | | | 0-300 | Valid Range | 424 | 84.63 |
| SYSTOLIC | Systolic Blood Pressure | Num 8 | 90-170 | Valid Range (units=mm Hg) | 501 | 100.00 |
| DIASTOLIC | Diastolic Blood Pressure | Num 8 | 60-110 | Valid Range (units=mm Hg) | 501 | 100.00 |
| HIGHBPMED | On High Blood Pressure Medication | Num 8 | 0 | Not on Medication | 391 | 78.04 |
| | | | 1 | On Medication | 110 | 21.96 |

**Data created for illustrating the *Data Detective's Toolkit*.**

# Index

# Ready to take your SAS® and JMP®skills up a notch?

Be among the first to know about new books,
special events, and exclusive discounts.
**support.sas.com/newbooks**

Share your expertise. Write a book with SAS.
**support.sas.com/publish**

Continue your skills development with free online learning.
**www.sas.com/free-training**

sas.com/books
*for additional books and resources.*

THE POWER TO KNOW®